Veritas Press

Dear Friends,

We hope this guide will be helpful as you study the Old Testament and Ancient Egypt this year. You are about to take a journey through the past where you can see God's providence, judgement, and provision for His people on a daily basis. Imagine being Noah as he labored over his ark for years, or Moses as he led God's people out of bondage. The Israelites were able to see God crush an entire civilization as He destroyed the Egyptians with plagues. Have you ever wondered why the Egyptians did not become the civilization that continued to develop instead Greece and Rome? Simply stated, God essentially destroyed them beginning with the plagues. God was faithful to His people through the years just as He is today. What a joy it is for young children to come to realize God's faithfulness as they learn from the past.

There are 32 events/people featured in the cards in this series. That is approximately one per week. A few of the cards have extra projects which may spread into the following week. The projects are only suggestions, so use your imagination and have fun with your group. You will note that the projects vary to appeal to different ages. You may choose the ones you think are appropriate for your student(s). We recommend singing the song daily for the first several weeks, after that three times a week is usually enough. Remember, the reason for the song is to help memorize the chronology of the events. It is also good to have the children recite events, in proper order, rather than singing it after the song has been memorized. A sample school week might be planned as follows:

Monday: Sing the song (you may want to have a student come to the front of the room and hold up the flashcards in order as the class sings). Present the new card. Read what it says on the back and discuss it. Allow different students to read it out loud if you can. Then allow the students to answer questions on the worksheet. The questions are based on information on the cards.

Tuesday: Sing the song. Orally review questions from this card's worksheet and from previous events. Obviously you cannot review every question every day, so do a sampling. Assign different children different sources from the resource list on the card and allow them to look up the information and share it with the class.

Wednesday: Sing the song. Orally review questions from the worksheet. Do one of the projects.

Thursday: Sing the song. Orally review from this week and previous weeks. Discuss how this card relates to those before it. Do another project, if there is one.

Friday: Give test. Use remaining time for class instruction and drill.

Having fun makes it easy to learn. Using the cards for games is one way. Ask the children to shuffle them and then see who can get their cards in order the fastest. Or have four to six students mix up their cards and then play Go Fish. This allows them to get familiar with the titles. Or you can get in a large room and see who can make their own timeline the fastest. A good way to drill questions in a classroom is to divide the children into two teams and ask questions in order. Teams receive a point for each right answer.

We have found one of the best ways to file the cards is to laminate them, punch a hole in the top right corner, and keep them on a large ring. The children can add the newest card and also have the previous cards handy. Another idea is to laminate them, put a Velcro strip on the card and on the wall, and start a timeline that children can put up and take down over and over again. An extra set of cards mounted at the end of the room for a reference time line is a good idea too.

In order to encourage children to read historical fiction related to classroom work, we suggest a book chart to show points earned for each book read by each student. Increasing the comprehension and accountability through brief written or oral summaries or book reports will provide numerous additional learning opportunities. After receiving a certain number of points we allow the child to have a special lunch with their teacher. You could have a mom bring in a special lunch or allow the winners to go out.

Each worksheet, test, or writing assignment should receive three grades, one each for Content, Grammar and Linguistics (Spelling).

Content: A grading scale you may find helpful is to count ten points for essay questions, five points for one sentence answers and two points for fill in the blank answers. The percentile grade will then be the total number of points achieved divided by the total number of points possible.

Grammar: The child should answer the questions in a complete sentence in which they first restate the question. For example: What is the Scripture reference for Creation? The Scripture reference for Creation is Genesis 1-2. This grade should be applied to an application grade in grammar, but should not affect history content grades. We suggest application at twenty percent of the overall grade.

Linguistics: The children should spell all words correctly. You should deduct for misspelled words once the rule for spelling a particular word has been mastered. For example: i before e except after c. Once this has been covered a child's grade would be reduced if they spelled receive as recieve. If they are using a history card to do their worksheet they should be taught that those words to be transcribed directly from the card should be spelled correctly. This grade would be applied towards a linguistics application grade. Again we suggest twenty percent, but not to affect their history grade.

When you look at the tests you will see that there are not the same number of questions on each test or worksheet. We assign five points per question, with the listings of the chronology receiving two points per item listed. Partial credit may be counted because the questions are essay and they may have portions correct.

Some students may ask why they are receiving three grades on each paper. We believe that it is important for a student to realize that grammar and linguistics matter in history class as well as in grammar class. All three contribute to help make students understood by others, and are thus intertwined.

Finally we welcome your feedback and comments. We hope that his resource will enrich the education of those children entrusted to you, and will help them understand the comprehensive responsibility that God requires of them.

Sincerely,

Marlin and Laurie Detweiler
Veritas Press
September 15, 1998

OLD TESTAMENT AND ANCIENT EGYPT
Teachers Guide

TABLE OF CONTENTS

1. Creation
   a. Worksheet b01-1
   b. Project, Illustration of Creation b01-2,3
   c. Test b01-4

2. The Fall in the Garden
   a. Worksheet b02-1
   b. Project, Writing Exercise (Genesis 3) b02-2
   c. Test b02-3

3. Cain and Abel
   a. Worksheet b03-1
   b. Project, Writing Exercise (Genesis 4: 6,7) b03-2
   c. Test b03-3

4. The Flood
   a. Worksheet b04-1
   b. Project, The Ark b04-2,3
   c. Project II, Building the Ark b04-4
   d. Test b04-5,6

5. Tower of Babel
   a. Worksheet b05-1
   b. Project, Building the Tower b05-2
   c. Test b05-3,4

6. Unification of Upper and Lower Egypt by Pharaoh Menes
   a. Worksheet b06-1
   b. Project, Illustrated Hunting Expedition b06-2,3
   c. Project II, Salt Relief Map b06-4,5,6
   d. Project III, Crown b06-7,8
   e. Test b06-9

7. The Old Kingdom in Egypt
   a. Worksheet b07-1
   b. Project, Fresco b07-2,3,4
   c. Project II, Pyramid b07-5,6,7,8
   d. Test b07-9,10

8. First Intermediate Period in Egypt
   a. Worksheet b08-1
   b. Project, Isis and Osiris Mural b08-2
   c. Project II, Coloring Sheets b08-3,4
   d. Test b08-5,6

9. Call of Abram
   a.   Worksheet   b09-1
   b.   Project, Booklet of Traveling in Abram's Time   b09-2,3,4
   c.   Test   b09-5,6

10. God's Covenant with Abraham
   a.   Worksheet   b10-1
   b.   Project, Writing Project (Genesis 18)   b10-2
   c.   Test   b10-3,4

11. Hagar and Ishmael
   a.   Worksheet   b11-1
   b.   Project, Writing Exercise (Genesis 16 and 21)   b11-2
   c.   Test   b11-3,4

12. Sodom and Gomorrah
   a.   Worksheet   b12-1
   b.   Project, Newspaper Article   b12-2,3
   c.   Test   b12-4,5

13. Birth and Sacrifice of Isaac
   a.   Worksheet   b13-1
   b.   Project, Sacrifices Booklet   b13-2,3,4
   c.   Test   b13-5,6

14. The Middle Kingdom in Egypt
   a.   Worksheet   b14-1
   b.   Project, Hieroglyphics   b14-2,3
   c.   Test   b14-4,5

15. Joseph as a Slave
   a.   Worksheet   b15-1
   b.   Project, Dreams of Joseph   b15-2
   c.   Project II, Writing Exercise (Genesis 37)   b15-3
   d.   Test   b15-4,5

16. Famine in Egypt
   a.   Worksheet   b16-1
   b.   Project, Writing Exercise (Genesis 40)   b16-2
   c.   Project II, Sheaves   b16-3,4,5
   d.   Test   b16-6,7

17. The Twelve Tribes of Israel
   a.   Worksheet   b17-1
   b.   Project, High Priest   b17-2,3
   c.   Test   b17-4,5

18. Second Intermediate Period in Egypt
   a.   Worksheet   b18-1
   b.   Project, Mummy   b18-2,3,4
   c.   Test   b18-5,6

19. Code of Hammurabi
    a.   Worksheet   b19-1
    b.   Project, Cuneiform Tablet   b19-2
    c.   Test   b19-3

20. Hyksos Invasion of Egypt
    a.   Worksheet   b20-1
    b.   Project, Coloring Sheet   b20-2
    c.   Project, Chariot   b20-3,4,5,6
    d.   Test   b20-7,8

21. Early New Kingdom in Egypt
    a.   Worksheet   b21-1
    b.   Project, Senefer/Paddle Doll   b21-2,3,4,5,6
    c.   Test   b21-7,8

22. Moses' Birth
    a.   Worksheet   b22-1
    b.   Project, Writing Exercise (Exodus 2)   b22-2
    c.   Project II, Basket   b22-3
    d.   Test   b22-4,5

23. Plagues in Egypt
    a.   Worksheet   b23-1
    b.   Project, Letter   b23-2,3
    c.   Student Handout   b23-4
    d.   Teacher Information   b23-5
    e.   Project II, Match the Plague   b23-6,7
    f.   Test   b23-8,9

24. The Exodus
    a.   Worksheet   b24-1
    b.   Project, Writing Exercise (Exodus 14)   b24-2
    c.   Project, Moses, The Play   b24-3,4,5,6
    d.   Test   b24-7,8

25. Ten Commandments
    a.   Worksheet   b25-1
    b.   Project, Tablets   b25-2
    c.   Test   b25-3

26. Amenhotep IV and Monotheism
    a.   Worksheet   b26-1
    b.   Project, Coloring Sheet   b26-2
    c.   Test   b26-3,4

27. Reign of Tutankhamon
    a.   Worksheet   b27-1
    b.   Project, Literature Unit: Tut's Mummy, Lost… and Found   b27-2,3,4,5,6
    c.   Project II, Mask of Tutankhamon   b27-7,8
    d.   Project III, Video: King Tut, Tomb of Treasure   b27-9
    e.   Test   b27-10,11

28. Later New Kingdom in Egypt
    a.   Worksheet   b28-1
    b.   Project, Writing Exercise (Mortuary Temple, Ramses II)   b28-2
    c.   Project II, Video: Egypt: Quest for Eternity   b28-3
    d.   Test   b28-4

29. The Davidic Kingdom
    a.   Worksheet   b29-1
    b.   Project, Illustrate David's Life   b29-2
    c.   Project II, Writing Exercise (I Samuel 16)   b29-3
    c.   Test   b29-4,5

30. Solomon's Reign
    a.   Worksheet   b30-1
    b.   Project, Building the Temple   b30-2,3,4
    c.   Test   b30-5,6

31. Alexander the Great Conquers Egypt
    a.   Worksheet   b31-1
    b.   Project, Coloring Sheet   b31-2
    c.   Test   b31-3,4

32. Egypt Falls to Rome
    a.   Worksheet   b32-1
    b.   Project, Coloring Sheet   b32-2
    c.   Test   b32-3,4

Appendix

1. Literature Unit, The Pharaoh's of Ancient Egypt   Appendix 1-1 to 18

2. Bulletin Board Pattern   Appendix 2-1

3. An Egyptian Feast   Appendix 3-1,2,3,4

4. History Facts (who, what, where, when)   Appendix 4-1,2,3

CREATION
Worksheet

1. What book and chapters in the Bible cover the creation of the world?

    _____

    _____

2. How long has God existed?

    _____

    _____

3. Write what God created next to each day.

    Day 1: _____

    Day 2: _____

    Day 3: _____

    Day 4: _____

    Day 5: _____

    Day 6: _____

    Day 7: _____

CREATION
Project

Illustrate the seven days of Creation.

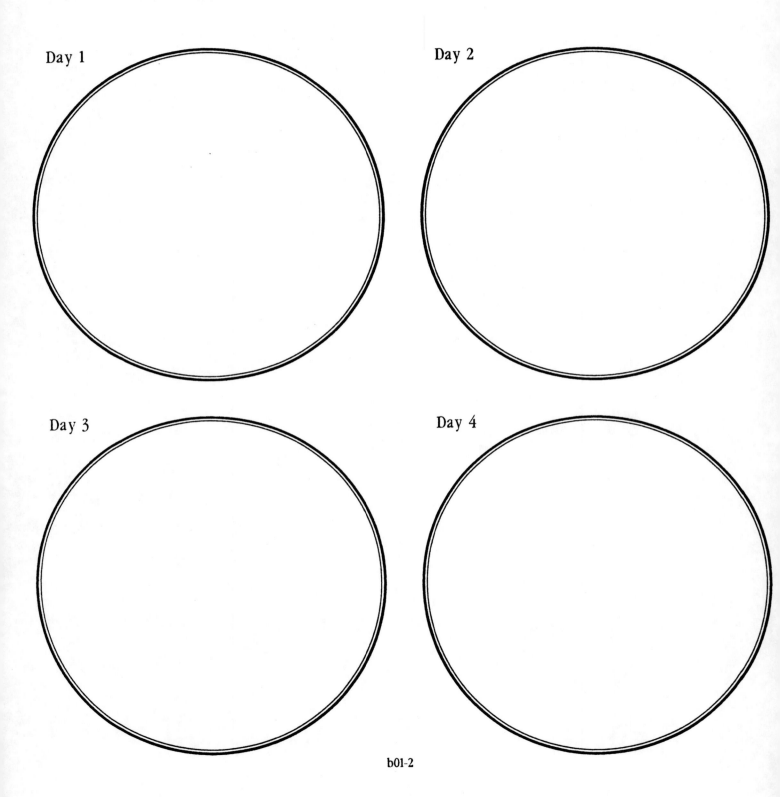

Day 1

Day 2

Day 3

Day 4

CREATION
Project, Page 2

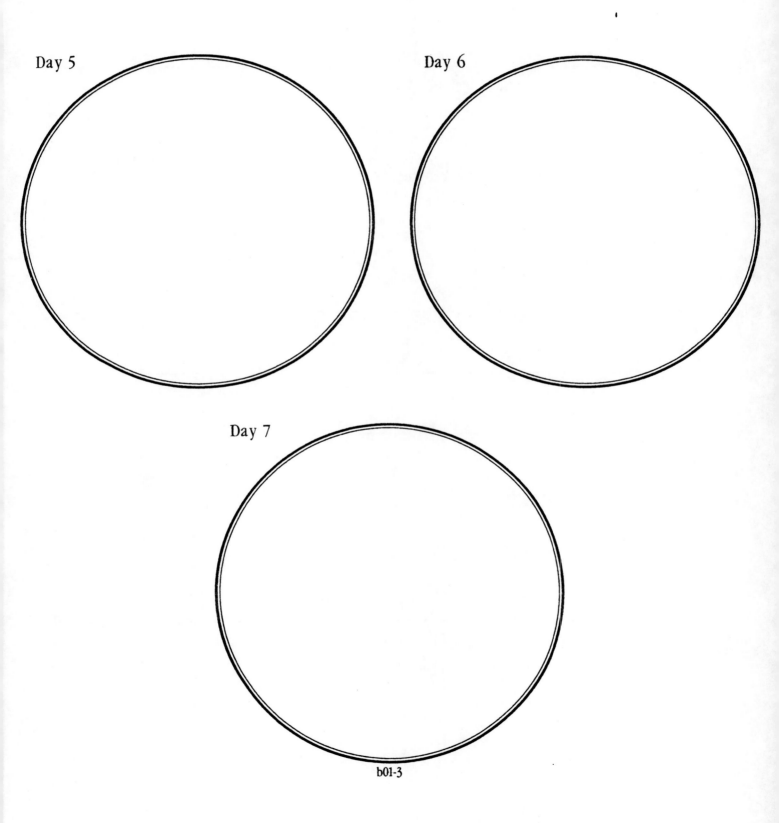

Day 5

Day 6

Day 7

CREATION
Test

1. Where can we find the story of Creation in the Bible?

   _____

   _____

2. Who existed before the world began?

   _____

   _____

3. Next to each day write what God created.

   Day 1:

   _____

   Day 2:

   _____

   Day 3:

   _____

   Day 4:

   _____

   Day 5:

   _____

   Day 6:

   _____

   Day 7:

   _____

THE FALL IN THE GARDEN
Worksheet

1. Who tempted Eve to eat of the Tree of the Knowledge of good and evil?

_____

_____

2. To whom did Eve offer the fruit? Did that person eat of the fruit also?

_____

_____

3. What was the earth like before the fruit was eaten?

_____

_____

4. What did God do when the forbidden fruit was eaten?

_____

_____

5. What was man's relationship with God like after the fruit was eaten?

_____

_____

_____

THE FALL IN THE GARDEN
Project

Read Genesis 3.

Using complete sentences, write a paragraph describing the Biblical meaning of the picture.

_____

_____

_____

_____

_____

_____

_____

_____

_____

_____

THE FALL IN THE GARDEN
Test

1. What did the serpent offer Eve?

   _____

   _____

2. What did Adam do when Eve offered him the fruit?

   _____

   _____

3. Why did God curse the ground and make life hard for mankind?

   _____

   _____

4. How was man's relationship with God changed after he sinned?

   _____

   _____

Review

1. Write what God created on each day.

   Day 1: _____

   Day 2: _____

   Day 3: _____

   Day 4: _____

   Day 5: _____

   Day 6: _____

   Day 7: _____

CAIN AND ABEL
Worksheet

1. Where is the story of Cain and Abel found in Scripture?

   _____

   _____

2. Who was the first child ever born? Who were his parents?

   _____

   _____

3. Who was Cain's brother?

   _____

   _____

4. What was the occupation of Cain? Of Abel?

   _____

   _____

5. What sacrifice did they each bring to God?

   _____

   _____

6. What was the purpose of sacrifices?

   _____

   _____

7. Who was the the world's first murderer? Why did he murder?

   _____

8. What was God's judgement on Cain?

   _____

   _____

CAIN AND ABEL
Project

So the Lord said to Cain, "Why are you angry? And why has your countenance fallen? If you do well, will you not be accepted? And if you do not do well, sin lies at the door. And its desire is for you, but you should rule over it." *(Genesis 4:6, 7)*

After discussing the meaning of these verses with your teacher write a paragraph below summarizing their meaning.

_____

_____

_____

_____

_____

_____

_____

_____

_____

_____

_____

_____

_____

_____

_____

_____

_____

CAIN AND ABEL

Test

In your own words write a paragraph retelling the story of Cain and Abel. Be sure to include all the important information.

_____

_____

_____

_____

_____

_____

_____

_____

_____

_____

_____

_____

_____

_____

_____

Review

1. Where in the Bible is the story of Creation?

   _____

2. Who tempted Eve to eat the forbidden fruit?

   _____

3. List the three events covered so far in chronological order.

   _____

   _____

   _____

THE FLOOD
Worksheet

1. Where is the flood described in the Bible?

   _____

   _____

2. Why was God grieved that He had made man?

   _____

   _____

3. God decided to destroy man. One man found favor in God's sight. Who was that man?
   And what did God instruct him to do?

   _____

   _____

4. What did God do to destroy man? For how long?

   _____

   _____

5. Define "covenant."

   _____

   _____

6. What was the purpose of the rainbow God sent after the flood?

   _____

   _____

THE FLOOD
Project

Noah was 480 years old when God called him to build the ark. It took Noah 120 years to complete the ark. How old would Noah have been? Imagine what it would have been like to work on the ark for 120 years waiting for the flood to come. Do you think people believed Noah when he told them that the earth was going to be covered with water?

The ark was bigger than we can imagine. It was larger than twelve school buses lined up in a row. If we were able to put the ark on a football field it would not fit in between the goal post as it was about 1 1/2 times as large as a football field. Noah's ark was 450 feet long, 75 feet wide, and about 45 feet high.

Noah was faithful to God year after year as he labored to do what God had called him to do. What lesson can we learn from this as we labor to do God's work in our own lives?

THE FLOOD
Project, Page 2

Color this.

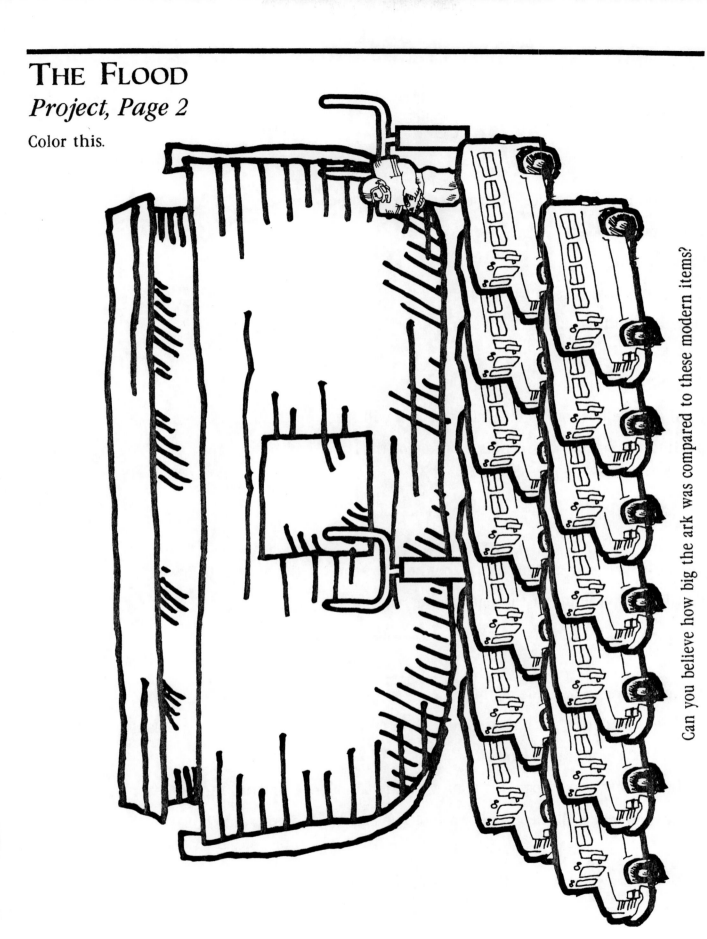

Can you believe how big the ark was compared to these modern items?

THE FLOOD
Project 2

Supplies

two shoe boxes with lids, one smaller than the other

white poster board

brown paint

miscellaneous colors to paint animals

clay that will harden

Steps

1. Glue shoe lids to boxes. (A hot glue gun will speed up the process.)

2. Glue the smaller box centered on top of the larger box.

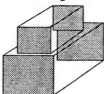

3. Out of poster board cut a roof for the ark according the pattern below.

    Glue it to the top of the top (smaller) box.

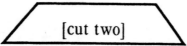

[cut two]

4. Cut a door in one side of the ark.

5. Paint the entire ark brown. (Older children may want to use a dark marker to make the "wood" have a granular look.)

6. Use clay to make Noah, his family, and the animals. Paint the animals after the clay has hardened. (Remember it was not two of every kind of animal. See Genesis 6:19 - 7:3)

This would also be a good time to distinguish between clean and unclean animals.

THE FLOOD
Test

1. Where in the Bible is the story of the flood found?

   _____

   _____

2. Why did God flood the earth?

   _____

   _____

3. Why did Noah find favor in God's sight?

   _____

   _____

4. What did God instruct Noah to do?

   _____

   _____

5. What covenant sign did God send? What did it mean?

   _____

   _____

Review

1. Why did God curse the ground and make life difficult for man?

   _____

   _____

   _____

2. What happened when Cain and Abel brought their sacrifices before the Lord?

_____

_____

3. Why did God curse Cain?

_____

_____

4. List the four events in chronological order covered to date and the Scripture references for them.

_____

_____

_____

_____

_____

_____

THE TOWER OF BABEL
Worksheet

1. Where in the Bible do you find the description of the Tower of Babel?

   _____

   _____

2. How many languages were spoken in the world before the Tower of Babel?

   _____

   _____

3. What did God cause to happen while the people built the Tower of Babel?

   _____

   _____

4. What do some archeologists believe may be the ruins of the Tower of Babel?

   _____

   _____

   _____

THE TOWER OF BABEL
Project

The Tower of Babel may have been a ziggurat, also known as a temple tower. The Egyptians may have gotten ideas for their pyramids by copying ziggurats. The tower is built by building small platforms; one on top of the other. They were probably constructed out of mudbricks which were made from mud and straw. In some instances each level was painted a different color and a shrine was placed at the top.

To see a picture of a ziggurat refer to The Children's Illustrated Bible, pages 28 and 29.

You can make a ziggurat in several ways. One, you can collect varying sizes of boxes so that they can be stacked one on top of the other progressively smaller. Two, you can construct a small clay model using various colors of clay. You may think of other ways, too.

THE TOWER OF BABEL
Test

1. Where in the Bible is the story of the Tower of Babel found?

   _____

   _____

2. How did we come to have many languages spoken in the world?

   _____

   _____

3. What do some archaeologist believe may be the ruins of the Tower of Babel?

   _____

   _____

Review

1. Next to each day write what God created.

   Day 1: _____

   Day 2: _____

   Day 3: _____

   Day 4: _____

   Day 5: _____

   Day 6: _____

   Day 7: _____

THE TOWER OF BABEL
Test, Page 2

2. When did sin enter the world?

_____

_____

3. Who was the first baby born into the world?

_____

_____

4. What was God's covenant with Noah?

_____

_____

5. In sequence write the events studied to date.

_____

_____

_____

_____

_____

_____

_____

_____

_____

_____

UNIFICATION OF UPPER AND LOWER EGYPT
Worksheet

1. Who was the first known Pharaoh of Egypt? How old was he when he became Pharaoh?

   _____

   _____

   _____

2. What remarkable feat did this Pharaoh accomplish?

   _____

   _____

   _____

3. What crown did this Pharaoh wear? What did it represent?

   _____

   _____

   _____

   _____

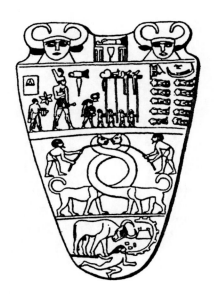 

UNIFICATION OF UPPER AND LOWER EGYPT
Project

Little is known about Menes. However, it is known that he was a mighty hunter. He hunted elephants, giraffes, lions and wild oxen with only a bow and arrow. In his little boat he would hunt hippopotami and crocodiles in the Nile River with harpoons and lances. He once chased an antelope over the desert leaving his men behind. He found himself being chased by a pack of half-wild dogs. To escape he dove into a lake and then faced the jaws of crocodiles before reaching safety.

How is such information known to us?

_____

_____

_____

On the following page illustrate pyramid paintings/reliefs depicting this story.

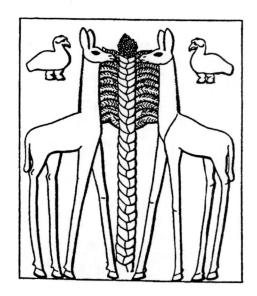

UNIFICATION OF UPPER AND LOWER EGYPT
Project, Page 2

Create illustrations of paintings/reliefs of the hunting expeditions of Pharaoh Menes

Unification of Upper and Lower Egypt

Project 2
Salt Relief Map: Instructions

Materials

Cardboard box lid for letter size (8.5" x 11")
paper (available from printing companies)
Copy of map of Egypt (next page)

White glue

Pencil

Two mixing bowls

Mixing spoon

Measuring cups

Flour

Salt

Water

Food coloring

Recipe for Making Three Maps

6 cups of salt

6 cups of flour

2-3 cups of water

Combine salt and flour, mix well. Add two cups of water and mix until smooth. Add remaining water as needed. Divide dough in half. Add green food coloring to one portion and blue to the other. Cover and set aside. (This can be mixed the day before and stored in a refrigerator. It may also be frozen to use later.)

Instructions

1. Looking at the map on the following page draw the Mediterranean Sea, Red Sea, and Nile River on the inside of the box lid.
2. Using blue dough, cover the bodies of water except the Nile River.
3. Using green dough cover the land areas including the Nile River.
4. Locate Upper and Lower Egypt. Referring to the map on the following page, carve out the Nile River with a pencil.
5. Push blue dough into the Nile River area with a pencil.
6. Allow one week for drying.
7. After drying cut labels out and glue them in the appropriate places.

Labels—

Mediterranean Sea

Red Sea

Lower Egypt

Upper Egypt

Memphis

UNIFICATION OF UPPER AND LOWER EGYPT

Project 2, Page 2

Map

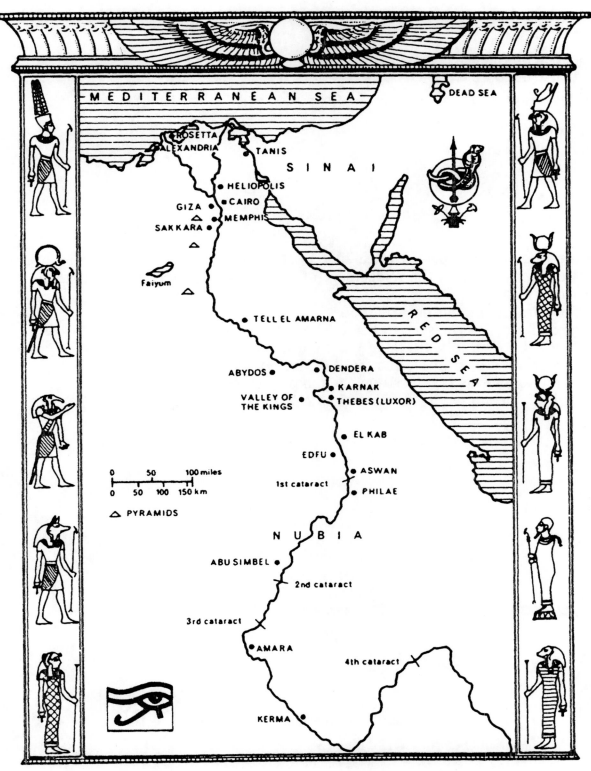

UNIFICATION OF UPPER AND LOWER EGYPT

Project 3

Crown of Upper and Lower Egypt

Supplies

Red construction paper (12" x 18")
White construction paper
Yellow construction paper
Stapler
Scotch tape
Scissors
Poster board

Directions

Trace the patterns onto poster board and cut them out to make a permanent pattern.
Place the poster board on the folded edge of red and white paper as noted on the
pattern provided herein.
Trace the pattern and cut out the shape.
Use scraps of red, as necessary to size the pattern to fit each child.
Staple the red crown so it fits snugly around the head of each child.
Staple the white crown inside the front of the red crown. Cut a slit
in the white crown so as to position the tab of the yellow serpent
on the white portion of the crown and glue or tape it in place.

Place this edge on the fold.

Cut from red construction paper.

UNIFICATION OF UPPER AND LOWER EGYPT

Project 3, Page 2

Crown of Upper and Lower Egypt

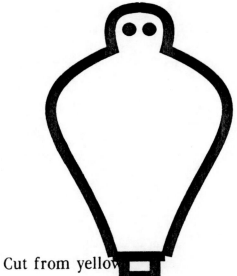

Cut from yellow construction paper.

Cut from white construction paper.

Place this edge on the fold.

UNIFICATION OF UPPER AND LOWER EGYPT
Test

1. Who was the first known Egyptian Pharaoh?

   _____

   _____

2. At what age did he become Pharaoh?

   _____

   _____

3. What important feat did this Pharaoh accomplish?

   _____

   _____

4. What crown did this Pharaoh wear? Why did he wear it?

   _____

   _____

Review

1. What had God forbidden of Adam and Eve?

   _____

   _____

2. How did man fall out of fellowship with God?

   _____

3. Who was the first baby ever born?

   _____

4. After the Flood God made a covenant with Noah. What was that covenant?

   _____

   _____

5. On the back list all events covered in chronological order with Biblical references where applicable.

THE OLD KINGDOM IN EGYPT
Worksheet

1. What is the age when pyramids were built known as?

   _____

   _____

2. Why were so many pyramids able to be built during this time period?

   _____

   _____

3. Name the largest pyramid built? For whom was it built?

   _____

   _____

4. How many men labored to build the largest pyramid? How long did it take to complete?

   _____

   _____

5. Why were the Pharaohs so concerned with building pyramids?

   _____

   _____

6. Does the Egyptian building of pyramids and storage of great wealth follow
   or violate Matthew 6:19—21? Why?

   _____

   _____

THE OLD KINGDOM IN EGYPT
Project

On the following two pages you will find information regarding the Book of the Dead. Copy each of these pages for your students and go over them orally in class. During the conversation continually remind them that the Egyptians were a sinful people who did not worship the living God of Scripture. After your class discussion the project below may be done.

Materials

plaster of Paris

styrofoam vegetable trays (most groceries stores have them)

pencil

water color paints

Mix plaster of Paris according to directions on package. Pour into foam tray, three quarters filled. Allow to dry. Draw an Egyptian picture as they might have used in the Book of the Dead. Using water colors paint the scene.

Many of the resources on the card have excellent images to look at for ideas.

THE OLD KINGDOM IN EGYPT
Project, Page 2

Book of the Dead

The Egyptian Book of the Dead was a collection of over 200 magic spells. Each spell was a prayer intended to help the person on their journey to the afterlife.

During the Old Kingdom the spells were inscribed on the walls of the pyramids. Later they were painted inside coffins and eventually on papyrus.

THE OLD KINGDOM IN EGYPT
Project, Page 3

Standing before Osiris, the god of rebirth, the soul must prove himself worthy to be sent on by saying these typical words from a Book of the Dead:

O ye lords of truth,

I have not secretly done evil against mankind;

I have not told falsehoods;

I have not made the laborer do more

than his daily task;

I have not been idle;

I have not been drunk;

I have not caused hunger;

I have not murdered;

I have not stolen;

I have not cheated the weight of the balance;

I have not slandered anyone.

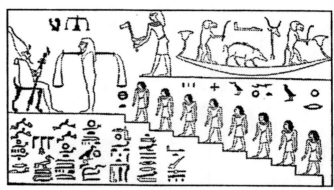

Egyptian Judgement Scene

Describe the similarity between the above words and the Ten Commandments of the Bible (Exodus 20).

_____

_____

_____

How do we actually secure life after death?

_____

_____

_____

THE OLD KINGDOM IN EGYPT
Project
Pyramids

Read the books *The Great Wonder* by Annabelle Howard, and one of the following: *Pyramid* by Macaulay, *Egyptian Pyramid* by Elizabeth Longley, or *Pyramids* a Scholastic, Inc. book.

Have children color the cover of this book. Make a copy of the pyramid book for each child and answer the comprehension questions. When this is done have the children cut out the pyramid shapes and staple them into a triangular book.

PYRAMIDS

THE OLD KINGDOM IN EGYPT
Project, Page 2
Pyramids

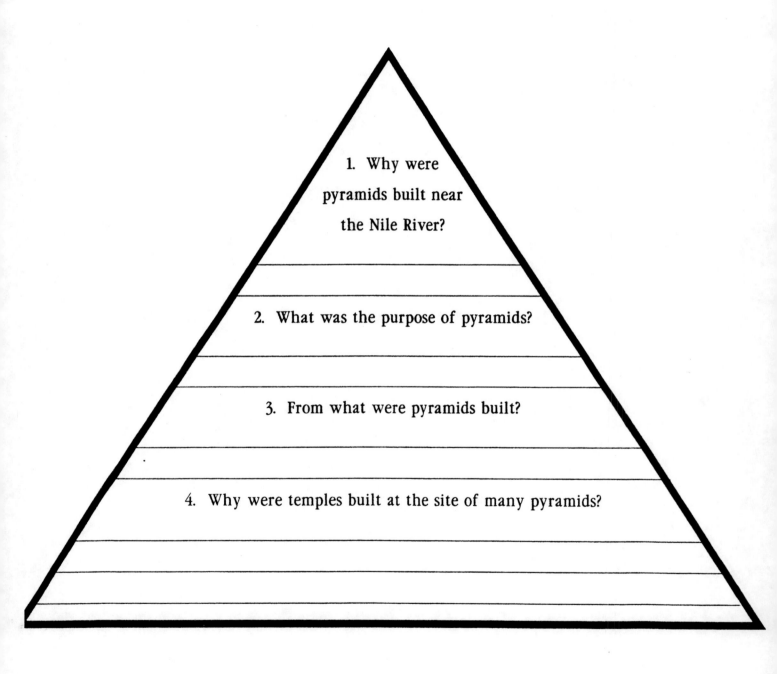

1. Why were pyramids built near the Nile River?

2. What was the purpose of pyramids?

3. From what were pyramids built?

4. Why were temples built at the site of many pyramids?

THE OLD KINGDOM IN EGYPT
Project, Page 3
Pyramids

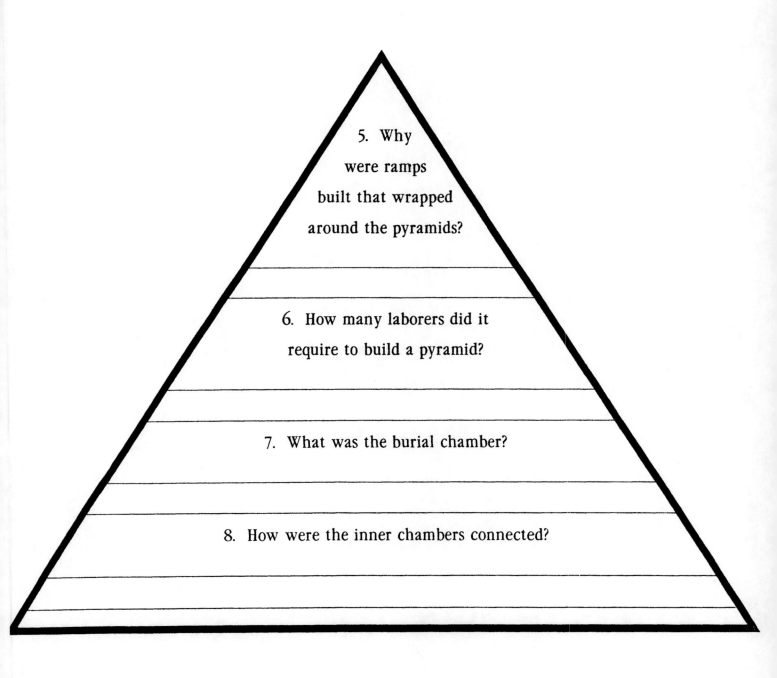

5. Why were ramps built that wrapped around the pyramids?

6. How many laborers did it require to build a pyramid?

7. What was the burial chamber?

8. How were the inner chambers connected?

THE OLD KINGDOM IN EGYPT
Project, Page 4
Pyramids

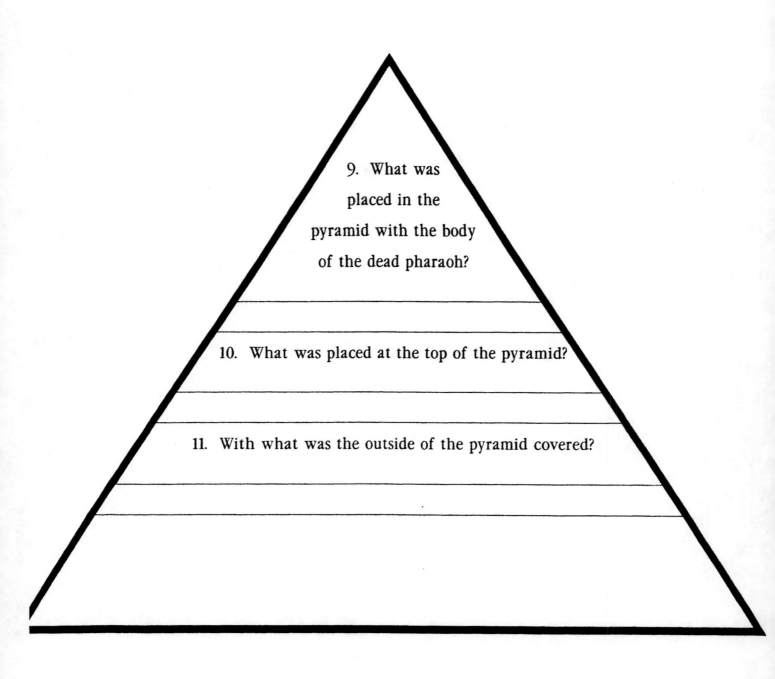

9. What was placed in the pyramid with the body of the dead pharaoh?

10. What was placed at the top of the pyramid?

11. With what was the outside of the pyramid covered?

THE OLD KINGDOM IN EGYPT

Test

1. For what is the Old Kingdom in Egypt known?

   _____

   _____

   _____

2. What were the conditions in Egypt during this period?

   _____

   _____

   _____

3. What was the largest of all pyramids? For whom was it built?

   _____

   _____

   _____

   _____

Review

1. What did God create on the second day of Creation?

   _____

   _____

2. Where in Scripture is the Fall found?

   _____

   _____

   _____

THE OLD KINGDOM IN EGYPT
Test

3. Who was the first baby born?

_____

_____

4. Why did God flood the earth?

_____

_____

5. Where is the Tower of Babel found in Scripture?

_____

_____

6. What is another name for Pharaoh Menes?

_____

_____

7. On the back write the events studied thus far in order. Include Biblical references where applicable.

FIRST INTERMEDIATE PERIOD
Worksheet

1. What are the approximate dates of the First Intermediate Period in Egypt?

   _____

   _____

2. With which dynasties does this period coincide?

   _____

   _____

3. What activity predominated during this period?

   _____

   _____

4. What happened to Egypt during this time?

   _____

   _____

   _____

An Egyptian Noble Hunting Wtih A Boomerang

FIRST INTERMEDIATE PERIOD
Project

During the First Intermediate Period Osiris, an Egyptian god, was designated as ruler of the dead. The Egyptians believed that an underworld existed. They called it Duatt. Parts of Duatt were full of lakes of fire, executioners and snakes. In order to reach the "land of perfect peace" they must journey before the hall of Osiris. Osiris sits on a throne of gold amid 42 solemn judges. Isis, his wife, sits by his side and Anubis, the jackal-headed god uses scales to weigh men's hearts. Standing before Osiris the soul must prove himself worthy to be sent on to Aalu. Read the chapter on Isis and Osiris in the *Tales of Ancient Egypt* and make a classroom mural showing the myth of Isis and Osiris. Hang white bulletin board paper on a wall and assign children different parts of the story:

1. The birth of Osiris.

2. The marriage of Isis and Osiris.
   (Point out the fact that this shows pharaohs marrying their own sisters.)

3. Ra's encounter with the cobra.

4. Isis, Ra, and the secret name.

5. Death of Ra.

6. Osiris, Pharaoh of Egypt.

7. Set's deception.

8. Isis in search of Osiris's body.

9. Temple of Baalat Gebal.

10. Burial of Osiris.

Remind children that this is not biblical Truth, but Egyptian mythology.

FIRST INTERMEDIATE PERIOD
Project

Color this picture

Tutankhamon in life (left) and as mummified Osiris (right).
Mural from tomb of Tutankhamon.

FIRST INTERMEDIATE PERIOD
Project

Color this picture

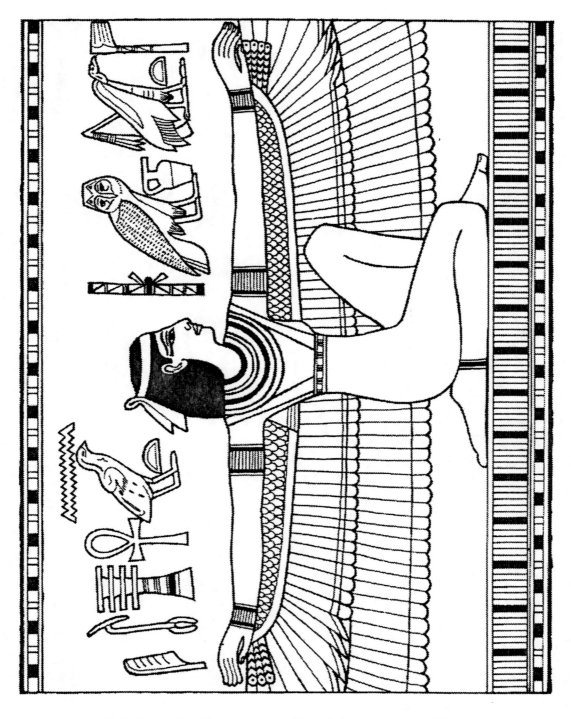

Isis in protective gesture. Mural from tomb of Seti

FIRST INTERMEDIATE PERIOD
Test

1. What were the approximate dates for the First Intermediate Period?

   _____

   _____

2. What dynasties coincide with this period?

   _____

   _____

3. Why did a civil war occur during this period?

   _____

   _____

Review

1. What happened on the seventh day of Creation?

   _____

   _____

2. What was the result of the Fall in man's relationship with God?

   _____

   _____

3. What was Cain's occupation? What was Abel's occupation?

   _____

   _____

4. Who was the one person who, with his family remained faithful to God immediately prior to the Flood?

   _____

5. At what point was more than one language spoken?

   _____

THE CALL OF ABRAM
Worksheet

1. What did God tell Abram to do when he was 75 years old?

   _____

   _____

2. What did God promise (covenant with) Abram?

   _____

   _____

3. Who accompanied Abram on his journey?

   _____

   _____

4. Where did Abram and his family settle?

   _____

   _____

5. What did God say He would do with the land where Abram settled?

   _____

   _____

6. What is the approximate date of the call of Abram?

   _____

   _____

7. What is the Scripture reference for the call of Abram?

   _____

   _____

THE CALL OF ABRAM
Project

On the following pages you will find pictures to turn into a little book for each student. The book will tell about the kind of life Abram, Sarai, and their family lived.

Supplies
Scissors

Glue

Construction paper

Divide construction paper in half width wise. Cut in half. Fold the halves in two and staple together to form a book. Cut the pictures apart and glue onto the construction paper. Once this is done spend time discussing the times of Abram and Sarai.

TRAVELING IN Abram's Times

Abram and his family traveled from Ur to Canaan. They walked or rode on camels carrying all their worldly goods with them. They lived a nomadic life and would rise at daybreak, set forward with the sun and travel until mid afternoon.
2

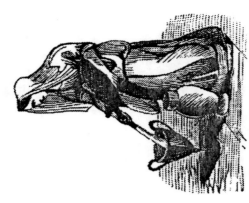

Water needed to be carried on the journey. Water would be drained from wells and put into bottles made from animal skins, which were sewn up leaving only one opening.
4

They dwelt in tents. The larger tents were divided into three apartments, the inner of which was given to the women and the outer to the servants with the young of the herds. Tents were originally built out of skins stretched upon poles. Linen was substituted later.
3

THE CALL OF ABRAM

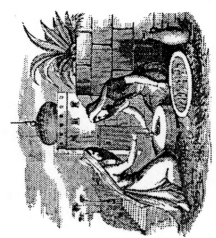

Few and simple were the household utensils. A hand-mill consisted of two stones; an upright handle turned the upper upon the lower, while the grain was put in through a central hole. Only women ground the grain.
6

Unleavened bread was a staple of their diet. Sarai may have prepared meals of unleavened bread, milk, and veal. Since Moses and the law as found in Leviticus came later, serving milk and meat at the same meal was not prohibited yet.
8

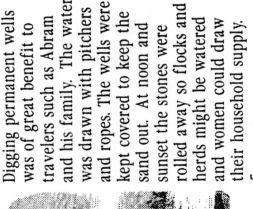

Digging permanent wells was of great benefit to travelers such as Abram and his family. The water was drawn with pitchers and ropes. The wells were kept covered to keep the sand out. At noon and sunset the stones were rolled away so flocks and herds might be watered and women could draw their household supply.
5

Butter and curdled milk were favorite dishes of the Israelites. The churning was done by putting curdled milk in a goat skinned bag which, being tied to a tent pole, was constantly moved back and forth until butter formed.
7

THE CALL OF ABRAM
Test

1. Where in Scripture is the Call of Abram recorded?

   _____

   _____

2. How old was Abram when God promised to make a great nation from his descendants? How many children did he have at the time?

   _____

   _____

3. . Where did God have Abram settle?

   _____

4. Who went with Abram on his journey to the new land?

   _____

   _____

5. What did God promise to do with this land?

   _____

   _____

6. What is the approximate date of the call of Abram?

   _____

Review

1. What did God create on the third day of Creation?

   _____

   _____

2. What happened to man as a result of the Fall?

   _____

   _____

THE CALL OF ABRAM
Test, Page 2

3. What is the biblical reference for Cain and Abel?

_____

_____

4. Who was the one person who, with his family, was saved from drowning during the flood?

_____

_____

5. Why did God cause the people to speak new languages at the Tower of Babel?

_____

_____

6. What happened during the Old Kingdom in Egypt?

_____

_____

7. List the events studied to date in chronological order.

_____

_____

_____

_____

_____

_____

_____

_____

_____

_____

GOD'S COVENANT WITH ABRAHAM
Worksheet

1. What was God's promise to Abram?

   _____

   _____

2. As part of the promise God changed Abram's and Sarai's names.

   What did their names become?

   _____

   _____

3. What did God tell Abraham about the covenant?

   _____

   _____

4. What was the sign of the covenant that God made?

   _____

   _____

5. What is the approximate date of God's covenant with Abraham?

   _____

   _____

6. Where in Scripture do we find the story of God's Covenant with Abraham?

   _____

   _____

GOD'S COVENANT WITH ABRAHAM
Project

Read Genesis 18.

Using complete sentences, write a paragraph describing the Biblical meaning in the picture.

_____

_____

_____

_____

_____

_____

_____

_____

_____

_____

_____

GOD'S COVENANT WITH ABRAHAM
Test

1. Where in scripture do we find the story of God's Covenant with Abraham?

   _____

   _____

2. What was the approximate date of God's Covenant with Abraham?

   _____

   _____

3. What was God's promise to Abraham?

   _____

   _____

4. What new names did God give Abram and Sarai?

   _____

   _____

5. To whom did God say the covenant would apply?

   _____

   _____

6. How was the covenant signified?

   _____

   _____

   _____

GOD'S COVENANT WITH ABRAHAM
Test, Page 2

Review

1. Fill in the days of Creation.

    Day 1: _____

    Day 2: _____

    Day 3: _____

    Day 4: _____

    Day 5: _____

    Day 6: _____

    Day 7: _____

2. With what did God tell Noah to fill the ark?

    _____

    _____

3. What happened during the First Intermediate Period in Egypt?

    _____

    _____

4. List the events studied to date in chronological order.

    _____

    _____

    _____

    _____

    _____

    _____

    _____

HAGAR AND ISHMAEL
Worksheet

1. What is the approximate date of the departure of Hagar and Ishmael?

   _____

   _____

2. What is the Scripture reference for the story of Hagar and Ishmael?

   _____

   _____

3. Why did Sarai ask Abram to take Hagar as his wife?

   _____

   _____

4. What was the name of the son born to Hagar and Abram?

   _____

   _____

5. What was the name of the son born to Abraham and Sarah?

   _____

   _____

6. Why did Sarah ask Abraham to cast Hagar and her son out
   and into the wilderness?

   _____

   _____

7. What did God promise Hagar?

   _____

   _____

   _____

   _____

HAGAR AND ISHMAEL
Project

Read Genesis 16 & 21.

Using complete sentences, write a paragraph describing the Biblical meaning in the picture.

_____

_____

_____

_____

_____

_____

_____

_____

_____

_____

_____

HAGAR AND ISHMAEL
Test

1. Where in Scripture do we find the story of Hagar and Ishmael?

   _____

   _____

2. Sarai had grown old and had not given birth to a child. What did she tell Abram to do?

   _____

   _____

3. What was the name of Abram and Hagar's child?

   _____

   _____

4. At the age of ninety Sarah had a child. What was the child's name?

   _____

   _____

5. What did Sarah ask Abraham to do with Hagar?

   _____

   _____

6. What was God's promise to Hagar?

   _____

   _____

Review

1. What is the Scripture reference for the flood?

   _____

2. What was the significance of the pyramids?

   _____

   _____

HAGAR AND ISHMAEL
Test, Page 2

3. What do we mean by the Call of Abram?

_____

_____

4. What is the scripture reference for God's Covenant with Abraham?

_____

_____

5. Write the events studied to date in chronological order.

_____

_____

_____

_____

_____

_____

_____

_____

_____

_____

_____

_____

SODOM AND GOMORRAH
Worksheet

1. What is the approximate date of the destruction of Sodom and Gomorrah?

   _____

   _____

2. Where in Scripture can we find the story of the destruction of Sodom and Gomorrah?

   _____

   _____

3. Why did Abraham plead with God not to destroy Sodom and Gomorrah?

   _____

   _____

4. Why did God save Lot?

   _____

   _____

5. What happened to Lot's wife?

   _____

   _____

6. Why was this event significant in Abraham's life?

   _____

   _____

   _____

   _____

   _____

SODOM AND GOMORRAH
Project

On the following page you will find a page from the Judea Chronicle. Pretend that you are a reporter for the paper and have just witnessed the destruction of Sodom and Gomorrah. Write an article for the paper reporting what you have seen. Remember to start with a topic sentence. Also, make sure that you use complete sentences.

JUDAH CHRONICLE

SODOM AND GOMORRAH
Test

1. What is the approximate date of the destruction of Sodom and Gomorrah?

   _____

   _____

2. Where in Scripture can we find the story of Sodom and Gomorrah?

   _____

   _____

3. Why did God destroy Sodom and Gomorrah?

   _____

   _____

4. When the cities of Sodom and Gomorrah were destroyed what happened to Lot and his family?

   _____

   _____

Review

1. What did the devil tempt Eve to do?

   _____

   _____

2. Why did Cain kill Abel?

   _____

   _____

3. Why did the Lord flood the earth?

   _____

   _____

4. What is the largest pyramid ever built?

_____

_____

5. Where in Scripture can we find the Call of Abram?

_____

_____

6. What promise did God make to Abram?

_____

_____

7. What was the name of Abraham and Hagar's son?

_____

_____

8. Write the events studied to date in chronological order.

_____

_____

_____

_____

_____

_____

_____

_____

_____

_____

BIRTH AND SACRIFICE OF ISAAC
Worksheet

1. What is the approximate date of the Birth and Sacrifice of Isaac?

_____

_____

2. Where in Scripture can we find the story of the Birth and Sacrifice of Isaac?

_____

_____

3. How old were Abraham and Sarah when Isaac was born?

_____

_____

4. When Isaac was a young boy what did God ask Abraham to do?

_____

_____

5. Why did an angel of the Lord appear to Abraham?

_____

_____

6. Why was God pleased with Abraham?

_____

_____

7. What can we learn about Abraham's faithfulness to God?

_____

_____

_____

_____

_____

BIRTH AND SACRIFICE OF ISAAC
Project

On the following pages you will find pictures to turn into a little book for each student. The book will explain the Old Testament sacrificial system.

Supplies

Scissors

Glue

Construction paper

Colored markers or crayons

Read through the following two pages with the children. Discuss the meaning and purpose of sacrifices with particular emphasis on the fact that Christ was the perfect sacrifice ending the need for future sacrifices.

Have the children illustrate the different types of sacrifices. Divide construction paper in half width wise. Cut in half. Fold the halves in two and staple together to form a book. Cut the pictures apart and glue onto the construction paper.

Sacrifices
—An Offering to God
Leviticus 1-8

A sacrifice was the method used in the Old Testament to ask forgiveness for sin or to give thanks and praise to God. Scripture teaches that God is Holy and cannot overlook sin, but that sin must be punished. Before Christ, sacrifices of animals and grain were offered to God to atone for sin. However, these sacrifices were imperfect and pointed toward the perfect sacrifice of Christ on the cross.

Altars were made of unhewn stones and later from hewn stones and metal. An altar was not only a place to offer a sacrifice. The word altar means "to approach." Consequently, stepping up to the altar was symbolic of communion with God and an act of remembering His covenant.

2

Only "clean" animals were allowed as sacrifices. These generally included sheep, goats, cattle, or doves. A grain offering (usually offered with an animal sacrifice) consisted of wheat flour mixed with olive oil, incense, and salt. It was mixed, then baked, fried, or cooked. It symbolized the person's dedication to God.

The "first fruits" were offerings of grain from the first harvest of the year. These offerings differed from other grain offerings in that they were full green heads of grain roasted on the fire. The first fruits were offered to God to give thanks for what He had provided.

On the following pages illustrate the offering described at the top of each page.

3

Burnt Offering
The whole animal less the skin was burned symbolizing the total giving of one's self to God.

4

Grain Offering

Wheat flour mixed in olive oil, incense, and salt. The mixture was then cooked and symbolized the worshippers dedication to God by giving God of his goods.

5

Peace Offering

The fatty parts of the animal were burned as a sign of fellowship with God. It was unusual in that the priest and the family ate much of the remaining meat.

6

Sin Offering

An animal was killed. Its blood was sprinkled on the altar as an atonement for one's sin.

7

Trespass Offering

Similar to the sin offering, this offering was for sins of omission, inadvertence or rashness. The fatty parts of the animal were burned and the priests kept the remaining meat. The poor were permitted to offer flour.

8

BIRTH AND SACRIFICE OF ISAAC
Test

1. What is the approximate date of the Birth and Sacrifice of Isaac?

   _____

   _____

2. Where in Scripture can we find the story of the Birth and Sacrifice of Isaac?

   _____

   _____

3. How was God's promise of a great nation finally fufilled through Abraham?

   _____

   _____

4. How did God test Abraham's faith?

   _____

   _____

5. Why did an angel of the Lord appear to Abraham?

   _____

   _____

Review

1. What did God do at the Tower of Babel?

   _____

   _____

2. Who unified Upper and Lower Egypt?

   _____

3. What happened during the First Intermediate Period?

   _____

   _____

BIRTH AND SACRIFICE OF ISAAC
Test, Page 2

4. What was the covenant God made with Abraham?

_____

_____

5. What happened to Hagar and Ishmael once they were cast into the wilderness?

_____

_____

6. Why did God destroy Sodom and Gomorrah?

_____

_____

7. List the chronology that you have studied to date. Provide Scripture references for biblically recorded events.

_____

_____

_____

_____

_____

_____

_____

_____

_____

_____

_____

_____

_____

THE MIDDLE KINGDOM IN EGYPT
Worksheet

1. What is the approximate date of the Middle Kingdom in Egypt?

   _____

   _____

2. What was the name of the Theban who seized control of Egypt during the 12th dynasty?

   _____

   _____

3. What cultural advances were made during the Middle Kingdom?

   _____

   _____

4. What Biblical event overlaps with the Middle Kingdom?

   _____

   _____

5. Who was the most important king/pharaoh of the 12th dynasty and why?

   _____

   _____

   _____

THE MIDDLE KINGDOM IN EGYPT
Project
Hieroglyphics

We owe most of our knowledge of Ancient Egypt to the inscriptions and manuscripts written in characters called hieroglyphics. This curious style of writing consisted of pictures or symbols representing words or letters. Thus, a circle stood for the sun, a crescent for the moon, an oval figure for the mouth, etc. As different pictures or signs were often used to represent the same word or sound, it is not strange that many centuries passed before scholars were able to decipher the hieroglyphic text. It was not until after 1799 that any clue to their meaning was discovered. In that year the finding of the Rosetta Stone gave the first key to the reading of hieroglyphics. On this stone the same inscription was given in three different sets of characters; the hieroglyphics, the demotic text (a briefer and more running form of hieroglyphics, commonly used in the papyri or manuscripts), and the Greek. By comparing the letters in certain Greek proper names with the letters of the same words in the Egyptian texts, the sounds for which the Egyptian characters stood were discovered.

Eventually, as hieroglyphic writing developed, most of the signs took on phonetic values. They could be used to stand for sounds and used with other hieroglyphs to spell out words.

Make several copies of the next page for each student. Have the students cut them apart and use the hieroglyphics to write a sentence by pasting the letters on construction paper as words. Have the students exchange them to translate another student's work.

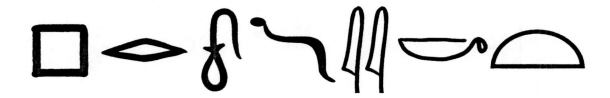

Project, Page 2

Hieroglyphics

THE MIDDLE KINGDOM IN EGYPT
Test

1. What is the approximate date of the Middle Kingdom in Egypt?

   _____

   _____

2. What did Amenemhet do during his reign?

   _____

   _____

3. What cultural advances were made during the Middle Kingdom?

   _____

   _____

4. Who was sold into slavery during this period?

   _____

   _____

5. Who was the most important king of the 12th dynasty and why?

   _____

   _____

   _____

THE MIDDLE KINGDOM IN EGYPT
Test

Review

1. What happened on the seventh day of Creation?

   _____

   _____

2. Why did God curse Cain?

   _____

   _____

3. What was built during the Old Kingdom in Egypt?

   _____

   _____

4. What did God call Abram to do?

   _____

   _____

5. What covenant did God make with Abraham?

   _____

   _____

6. Write the events studied to date in chronological order (continue on back).

   _____

   _____

   _____

   _____

   _____

   _____

   _____

   _____

JOSEPH AS A SLAVE
Worksheet

1. What is the Scriptural reference for Joseph as a Slave?

   _____

   _____

2. What is the approximate date of Joseph's slavery?

   _____

   _____

3. Why did Joseph's brothers envy him?

   _____

   _____

4. What did Joseph's brothers do to him?

   _____

   _____

5. What did Potiphar do to Joseph?

   _____

   _____

6. Why was Joseph put in prison?

   _____

   _____

7. What responsibility was Joseph given while in prison?

   _____

   _____

8. What remarkable feat did he accomplish while in prison?

   _____

   _____

JOSEPH AS A SLAVE
Project

In the "thought clouds"
illustrate Joseph's two dreams
from Genesis 37.

JOSEPH AS A SLAVE
Project

Read Genesis 37.

Using complete sentences, write a paragraph describing the Biblical meaning in the picture.

_____

_____

_____

_____

_____

_____

_____

_____

_____

_____

JOSEPH AS A SLAVE
Test

1. What did Joseph dream at the age of seventeen?

   _____

   _____

2. Why did Joseph's brothers envy him?

   _____

   _____

3. What did Joseph's brothers do to him?

   _____

   _____

4. Who was Potiphar?

   _____

   _____

5. Why was Joseph put in prison?

   _____

   _____

6. Whose dreams did Joseph interpret in prison?

   _____

   _____

7. What is the Scripture reference for Joseph as a Slave?

   _____

8. What is the approximate date for Joseph as a Slave?

   _____

   _____

JOSEPH AS A SLAVE
Test, Page 2

Review

1. List what God created on each of the seven days.

   Day 1: _____

   Day 2: _____

   Day 3: _____

   Day 4: _____

   Day 5: _____

   Day 6: _____

   Day 7: _____

2. After Cain killed Abel what was God's judgment on him?

   _____

   _____

3. What did God command Noah to do?

   _____

   _____

4. What was the purpose of the pyramids?

   _____

   _____

5. What is the Scripture reference for God's Covenant with Abraham?

   _____

6. On the back of this page list all events covered to date in chronological order.

FAMINE IN EGYPT
Worksheet

1. Why did Pharaoh summon Joseph from prison?

   _____

   _____

2. What were Joseph's interpretations of Pharaoh's dreams?

   _____

   _____

3. What job did Pharaoh give to Joseph?

   _____

   _____

4. What did Joseph do to ensure that there would be food during times of famine?

   _____

   _____

5. Who came to visit Joseph during the famine?

   _____

   _____

6. What eventually happened to Joseph and his family?

   _____

   _____

   _____

FAMINE IN EGYPT
Project

Read Genesis 40.

Using complete sentences, write a paragraph describing the Biblical meaning in the picture.

_____

_____

_____

_____

_____

_____

_____

_____

_____

_____

FAMINE IN EGYPT
Project 2

Signet Rings

When Pharaoh made Joseph second in command he took his signet ring off his hand and put it on Joseph's. He clothed him in garments of fine linen and put a gold chain around his neck. Giving Joseph the signet ring was very symbolic as it transferred power to him. A signet ring was used to sign documents. It would have been pressed into wax or clay as we sign our name to documents today.

Grain Crops

Egyptian farmers relied on the Nile River flooding its banks on a yearly basis. If this did not happen the soil would be too dry and infertile for any crops to grow and a famine would occur. Once the flood had subsided the first thing a farmer did was plow his fields with a wooden plow pulled by an ox. The farmer would then walk up and down the fields throwing seeds into the soil. Next the field was either plowed again or animals walked over the soil trampling the seeds into the ground. Once the grain had grown it had to be harvested. The crops were cut and tied into bundles (sheaves). They were then taken to the

PLOUGHING, HOEING AND SOWING. (*Description de l'Égypte. Pln.*)

GOATS TREADING IN GRAIN SOWN IN THE FIELD, AFTER THE WATER HAS SUBSIDED.

threshing floor where oxen or donkeys trampled them to separate the grain from the stalks. Now they were ready for a process called winnowing. The trodden grain was sifted and then thrown into the air, while a breeze was blowing, using a winnowing fork. The useful grain fell to the ground, but the lighter chaff blew away in the wind. The grain would be sifted through a sieve once more and placed into sacks in which to be stored.

Survival required much hard work in Egypt then. Joseph knew that he must store the grain at the granery if they were not to starve when the drought came and crops could not be grown.

FAMINE IN EGYPT
Project 2, Page 3

After reading the preceding page on the harvesting process and before beginning this project, have each child examine a stalk of wheat. Have each child take one stalk apart to see how difficult it was to separate the grain from the chaff. Then make the following decorative item.

Supplies

One small (3") terra-cotta pot per student

Dry foam

Paper twist ribbon

12 stalks of wheat per student

Hot glue gun

Directions

Cut, fit and hot glue foam into pot

Insert wheat into foam

Tie ribbon around the wheat

FAMINE IN EGYPT
Test

1. Why did Pharaoh summon Joseph from prison?

   _____

   _____

   _____

2. How did Joseph interpret Pharaoh's dreams?

   _____

   _____

   _____

3. What job did Joseph do for Pharaoh?

   _____

   _____

   _____

4. Who came to see Joseph during the famine? Did they know who he was?

   _____

   _____

   _____

5. What eventually happened to Joseph and his family?

   _____

   _____

   _____

   _____

FAMINE IN EGYPT
Test, Page 2

Review

1. What was Hagar's relationship to Sarai?

   _____

   _____

2. What covenant did God make with Abraham?

   _____

   _____

3. What occurred during the First Intermediate Period in Egypt?

   _____

   _____

4. Who unified Egypt and was the first known pharaoh?

   _____

   _____

5. List all events covered in chronological order. Where appropriate, list Bible references
   (continue on back).

   _____

   _____

   _____

   _____

   _____

   _____

   _____

   _____

   _____

THE TWELVE TRIBES OF ISRAEL
Worksheet

1. What promise had God made to Abraham?

   _____

   _____

   _____

   _____

2. To whom did God reveal this plan?

   _____

   _____

   _____

3. Who are the Patriarchs?

   _____

   _____

   _____

   _____

4. To what did God change Jacob's name? How many sons did he have?

   _____

   _____

5. What happened to each of Jacob's sons?

   _____

   _____

6. What are Jacob's descendants known as?

   _____

   _____

7. The _____ were God's _____ people.

THE TWELVE TRIBES OF ISRAEL
Project

Breastplate of the High Priest

Under the Mosaic law, the people were not allowed to offer sacrifices themselves to God; a priesthood was instituted to mediate between them and Jehovah. It was a royal priesthood. Aaron was the first High Priest and the office was passed down from father to son and assumed for a lifetime. The robes of glory in which Aaron was arrayed at his consecration, and in which he blessed Israel, are full of symbolic meaning. One of the articles of clothing the High Priest wore was the radiant Breastplate which had twelve of the most precious stones set in gold, and fixed upon the beautiful embroidery. The names of the tribes were cut on these stones, and the Breastplate was bound close to the heart of the High Priest. This represented the infinite compassion and love of Christ for His entire people, and the willingness to uphold His followers by the power of His might.

THE TWELVE TRIBES OF ISRAEL
Project, Page 2

Fill in the names of the twelve tribes of Israel and color the High Priest.

1. _____
2. _____
3. _____
4. _____
5. _____
6. _____
7. _____
8. _____
9. _____
10. _____
11. _____
12. _____

THE TWELVE TRIBES OF ISRAEL
Test

1. What is the Scripture reference for the Twelve Tribes of Israel?

   _____

2. What is the approximate date of the Twelve Tribes of Israel?

   _____

3. What promise did God make to Abraham?

   _____

   _____

4. To whom did God reveal much of the promise?

   _____

   _____

5. Who are the Patriarchs?

   _____

6. To what did God change Jacob's name? How many sons did Jacob have?

   _____

   _____

7. Name the twelve tribes.

   _____   _____

   _____   _____

   _____   _____

   _____   _____

   _____   _____

   _____   _____

8. What are the Jews known as?

   _____

   _____

The Twelve Tribes of Israel
Test, Page 2

Review

1. What may the ziggurat at Marduk be?

   _____

   _____

2. For whom was the great pyramid at Giza built?

   _____

   _____

3. What is the approximate date of the Call of Abram?

   _____

   _____

4. What was the name of the son born to Abram and Hagar?

   _____

   _____

5. Why did God destroy Sodom and Gomorrah?

   _____

   _____

7. What was the name of the son born to Abraham and Sarah?

   _____

   _____

8. On the back of this page list all events covered in chronological order.

SECOND INTERMEDIATE PERIOD IN EGYPT
Worksheet

1. What is the approximate date of the Second Intermediate Period in Egypt?

_____

_____

2. Of what dynasties did the Second Intermediate Period in Egypt consist?

_____

_____

3. How were rulers of this period characterized?

_____

_____

4. What was the role of local princes?

_____

_____

5. What land gains did Egypt make during this period?

_____

_____

_____

_____

_____

SECOND INTERMEDIATE PERIOD IN EGYPT
Project

Read the book *Mummies* by Aliki aloud to your class. This book provides detailed information on how the Egyptians cared for the dead through the entire burial process.

After reading the book have the students define the words on the following page. With younger students you may need to do this as a class and have them copy answers off the board. After you have done this the children may each make an Egyptian coffin.

Making an Egyptian Coffin
Supplies

White bulletin board paper

Tempera paint and brushes

Newspaper (a lot)

Stapler

Pencils

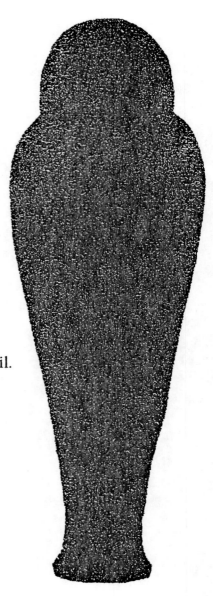

Directions

Have each child lie on his back on the bulletin board paper. Then have another child trace a coffin around him with a pencil. Cut out two of these shapes. Now draw designs on the coffin (refer to the book mentioned above for pictures).

SECOND INTERMEDIATE PERIOD IN EGYPT
Project, Page 2

Ba:

_____

_____

Mummified:

_____

_____

Fossil:

_____

_____

Decay:

_____

_____

Pharaoh:

_____

_____

Embalmer:

_____

_____

Natron:

_____

_____

Canopic jar:

_____

_____

SECOND INTERMEDIATE PERIOD IN EGYPT
Project, Page 3

Shroud:

_____

_____

Coffin:

_____

_____

Sarcophagus:

_____

_____

Funeral:

_____

_____

Mastabas:

_____

_____

Pyramid:

_____

_____

Shabtis:

_____

_____

SECOND INTERMEDIATE PERIOD IN EGYPT
Test

1. What is the approximate date of the Second Intermediate Period in Egypt?

   _____

   _____

2. Of what dynasties did the Second Intermediate Period in Egypt consist?

   _____

   _____

3. What was the character of the rulers during this period?

   _____

   _____

4. What areas did the local princes rule?

   _____

   _____

5. Of what major sites did Egypt gain control?

   _____

   _____

SECOND INTERMEDIATE PERIOD IN EGYPT
Test, Page 2

Review

1. What is the Scripture reference for the Fall in the Garden?

   _____

2. What covenant did God establish with Noah? What sign did he use to signify this?

   _____

   _____

3. Why did God cause man to speak different languages after the building of the tower of Bobel?

   _____

   _____

4. What is the Scripture reference for the Call of Abram?

   _____

   _____

5. What did God covenant with Abram?

   _____

   _____

6. Why did God destroy the cities of Sodom and Gomorrah?

   _____

   _____

7. On the back of this page list all events covered in chronological order.

CODE OF HAMMURABI
Worksheet

1. What is the approximate date of the Code of Hammurabi?

_____

_____

2. What land did Hammurabi rule?

_____

_____

3. What other landmarks are in this area?

_____

_____

4. Who was the sixth ruler of Babylon?

_____

_____

5. What kind of laws did Hammurabi establish?

_____

_____

6. How were these laws recorded?

_____

_____

_____

_____

CODE OF HAMMURABI
Project

Cuneiform is one of the earliest writings known to man. Once people started trading with one another they needed a way to keep track of their goods and payments. The Sumerians developed cuneiform to help them do this. Cuneiform, which also means wedge-shape, were characters that were wide at one end and pointed at the other. The characters were made by pressing what may have been a chopped off reed into a damp clay tablet.

Supplies

Air drying clay (such as DAS or Marblex)
Clay tools (available at art supply store)
Or you can use plastic knives

Directions

Give each student a handful of clay. Have them roll it into a ball and then flatten it into an oblong shape. After looking at the image of the clay tablet above have the students use their tools to make a replica of cuneiform writing. Place the tablets on a tray and allow them to dry.

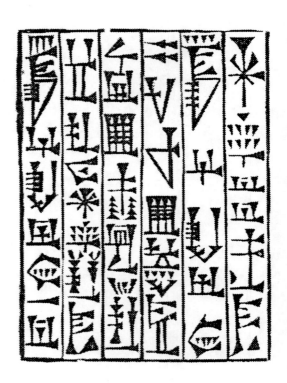

CODE OF HAMMURABI
Test

1. Who ruled the land of Babylonia?

   _____

   _____

2. What other landmarks are in the area of Babylonia?

   _____

   _____

3. What did the laws contain that Hammurabi established?

   _____

   _____

4. On what were the laws written?

   _____

   _____

5. What is the approximate date of the Code of Hammurabi?

   _____

   _____

Review

1. On the back write in chronological order all events covered to date.

   Include all dates and Scripture references available.

HYKSOS INVASION OF EGYPT
Worksheet

1. What is the approximate date for the Hyksos Invasion of Egypt?

   _____

   _____

2. What tools of battle did the Hyksos use that surprised the Egyptians?

   _____

   _____

3. From where did the Hyksos come?

   _____

   _____

4. Where did the Hyksos make their capital in Egypt after conquering it?

   _____

   _____

5. For how many years did the Hyksos rule Egypt?

   _____

   _____

Hyksos Invasion of Egypt
Project

Color this.

HYKSOS INVASION OF EGYPT
Project 2

Supplies

White card stock, 3 per student

Markers, colored pencils, and/or crayons

Brown or black yarn

Tape

White glue

Green clay

Shoe box lid

(A hot glue gun will be helpful)

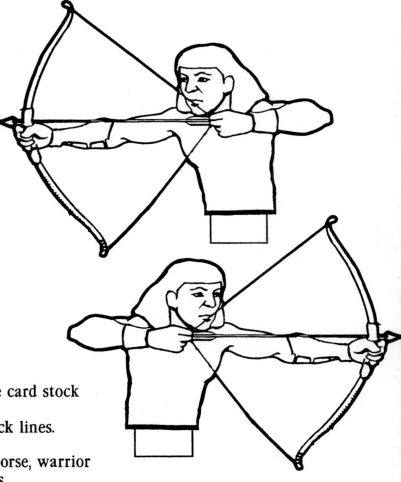

Directions
· Copy each page with patterns onto white card stock
    for each student.
· Color each item and cut along heavy black lines.
· Fold where indicated.
· Glue together the mirror images of the horse, warrior
    and wheels (do not cut the wheel pairs,
    but rather fold them).
· Cut the slit on the chariot top for the warrior and tape
    the chariot tabs in place.
· Put the warrior tab in the chariot slit and tap or glue in place.
· Glue or tape the blanket on the horse.
· Shape green clay to form a base in the shoe box top.
· Stabilize chariot and horse in the clay.
· Glue yarn "reins" from horse to chariot.

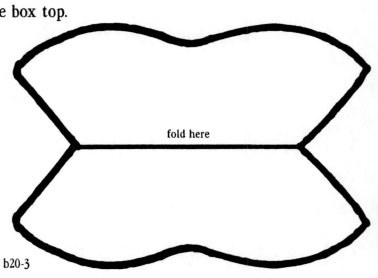

fold here

b20-3

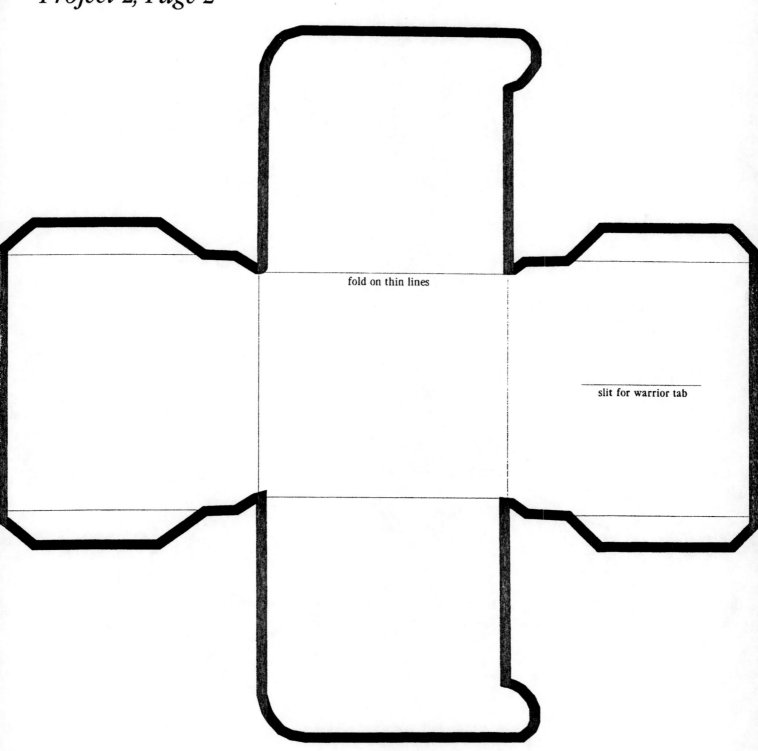

fold on thin lines

slit for warrior tab

HYKSOS INVASION OF EGYPT
Test

1. What is the approximate date of the Hyksos Invasion of Egypt?

   _____

   _____

   _____

2. What influence did the Hyksos have on the way Egyptians fought future battles?

   _____

   _____

   _____

3. What was the city of Avarias known for during the Hyksos occupation?

   _____

   _____

   _____

4. For how many years did the Hyksos rule Egypt?

   _____

   _____

   _____

   _____

   _____

   _____

HYKSOS INVASION OF EGYPT
Test, Page 2

Review

1. What is the Scripture reference for the Fall in the Garden?

   _____

   _____

2. Why did God cause the earth to flood?

   _____

   _____

3. List what God created on the seven days of Creation.

   _____

   _____

4. Where did God call Abram to go at the age of 75?

   _____

   _____

5. List the events studied to date in chronological order.

   _____

   _____

   _____

   _____

   _____

   _____

   _____

   _____

   _____

EARLY NEW KINGDOM IN EGYPT
Worksheet

1. What is the approximate date of the Early New Kingdom in Egypt?

_____

_____

2. Of what dynasty did the Early New Kingdom consist?

_____

_____

3. Who did the Egyptian army defeat in 1570 BC? What did the Egyptians learn from these people?

_____

_____

4. What is the name of the pharaoh that led the Egyptians in their defeat?

_____

_____

5. What is the name of the Egyptian princess who may have found Moses in the Nile?

_____

_____

6. Who was the first Egyptian woman to rule Egypt? How did she gain control of Egypt?

_____

_____

7. Who may have been the Pharoah of the Exodus?

_____

_____

8. What gods were worshipped during this dynasty?

_____

Aton

EARLY NEW KINGDOM IN EGYPT
Project

Senefer, a Young Genius in Old Egypt

Either read aloud or have your students read the book titled *Senefer, a Young Genius in Old Egypt* by Beatrice Lumpkin. *Senefer* is an exciting story of a little boy in Ancient Egypt. Although this book has multicultural tendencies, we believe that it is a good book to use when reading about Egypt. On the following page you will find questions about the book *Senefer*. Following the questions you will find a pattern for an Egyptian paddle doll, and a handout on ancient Egyptian toys.

Supplies

1/4 inch plywood or foam board

Small paint brushes

Paint

Black yarn

Beads

Drill

Saw

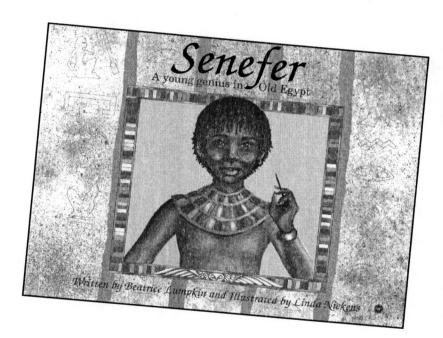

Directions

· Copy the outline of the paddle doll onto the plywood or foam board and cut out
  using appropriate tools.

· Drill holes in the head for the hair.

· Allow children to paint the paddle dolls as they like.

· Then tie yarn on for hair.

· They may want to tie beads onto the yarn after placing it in the hair.

EARLY NEW KINGDOM IN EGYPT
Project, Page 2

1. Who was Senefer?

   _____

   _____

2. Why did the children in Egypt wear very little clothing?

   _____

   _____

3. Where were Senefer and his mother going?

   _____

   _____

4. What was the black earth?

   _____

   _____

5. How did some people pay Nefert for her dolls?

   _____

   _____

6. What do these symbols represent? //////////∩∩

   _____

   _____

7. Who were the scribes?

   _____

   _____

8. Why were the scribes impressed with Senefer?

   _____

   _____

9. What happened to Pepi?

_____

_____

10. Where did they find Pepi?

_____

_____

11. Where was Senefer invited to attend?

_____

_____

12. What did Nefert paint on the lid of the box for Senefer? What did it represent?

_____

_____

13. What were the boats carrying?

_____

_____

14. Who was Hatshepsut?

_____

_____

15. What was the purpose of the obelisks?

_____

_____

16. What did Senefer grow up to be?

_____

_____

EARLY NEW KINGDOM IN EGYPT
Project, Page 4

Senefer, a Young Genius in Old Egypt
Answers

1. An African boy who lived in Egypt.
2. The days were very hot so they wore little clothing.
3. They were on their way to the market to sell dolls.
4. It was the rich soil where they grew their food.
5. Some people payed with loaves of bread.
6. Egyptian numbers.
7. People who made their living by writing.
8. Because he was able to write and add numbers.
9. He was missing.
10. He was asleep under a white cloth used to cover the bread at their market stand.
11. The scribes school.
12. A beautiful bird, the ibis who was the Egyptian God of the Scribes.
13. They brought two obelisks, made of stone each thirty meters long.
14. The Pharaoh.They were to point the way to the Egyptian Sun god.
15. He became one of Egypt's greatest mathematicians and builders.
    He designed the greatest temple in all of Egypt.

EARLY NEW KINGDOM IN EGYPT
Project, Page 4

Egyptian Paddle Doll

Egyptian children were no different than children today. They liked toys and liked to play. Evidence of balls, rattles, animals on wheels, dolls and games such as senet have been found as archeologist's have uncovered the past.

One of the favorite toys were paddle dolls. These dolls were made of wood and some times had a bead head with hair attached. The dolls were painted with geometric designs. Although we may never know this, paddle dolls may have been placed in tombs to act as companions in the afterlife.

EARLY NEW KINGDOM IN EGYPT
Test

1. What is the approximate date of the Early New Kingdom in Egypt?

   _____

   _____

2. Of what dynasty did the Early New Kingdon consist?

   _____

   _____

3. How do Moses and Hatshepsut relate to one another?

   _____

   _____

4. Who was the first woman pharaoh?

   _____

   _____

5. Who may have been the pharaoh of the Exodus?

   _____

   _____

6. Who were Amon and Aton?

   _____

   _____

Review

1. What did God create on the fifth day of creation?

   _____

2. Who tempted Eve to eat of the tree of knowledge of good and evil?

   _____

3. Who were Cain and Abel's parents?

_____

_____

4. Who was the first person to unify Upper and Lower Egypt?

_____

_____

5. What was the largest of all pyramids?

_____

_____

6. What happened during the First Intermediate Period in Egypt?

_____

_____

7. What did God call Abram to do when he was 75 years old?

_____

_____

8. What did Sarah ask Abraham to do to Hagar and Ishmael?

_____

_____

9. On the back of this page list all events covered in chronological order.

MOSES' BIRTH
Worksheet

1. Why did the new pharaoh (maybe Thutmose I) fear the Israelites?

   _____

   _____

2. What order did the new pharaoh give because of his fear?

   _____

   _____

3. What happened to Moses shortly after his birth?

   _____

   _____

4. Why was Moses now safe?

   _____

   _____

5. What did the royal family not know about Moses?

   _____

   _____

MOSES' BIRTH
Project

Read Exodus 2.

Using complete sentences, write a paragraph describing the Biblical meaning in the picture.

_____

_____

_____

_____

_____

_____

_____

_____

_____

_____

MOSES' BIRTH
Project 2

In Biblical times baskets had many purposes. They were made from papyrus, a triangular shaped reed. They would grow about 13 feet tall along the banks of the Nile River. They were woven by craftsmen called weavers or by women at home.

Moses' mother may have woven the basket in which he was placed. You may want to have your students make a basket from reeds. Kits and instructions for doing this may be ordered from:

Frank's Cane and Rush Supply
7252 Heil Avenue
Huntington Beach, CA 92647
tel: 714-847-0707
fax: 714-843-5645
www.franksupply.com

MOSES' BIRTH
Test

1. What is the approximate date of Moses' Birth?

   _____

   _____

2. What is the Scripture reference for Moses' Birth?

   _____

   _____

3. Why did the new pharaoh fear the Israelites?

   _____

   _____

4. What did the new pharaoh order the Israelite midwifes to do?

   _____

   _____

5. What did Moses' mother do to save his life?

   _____

   _____

6. What kind of life did Moses live until he turned 40?

   _____

   _____

Moses' Birth
Test, Page 2

Review

1. What occurred during the First Intermediate Period?

   _____

   _____

2. What promise did God make to Abram?

   _____

   _____

3. Why was Sarah jealous of Hagar?

   _____

   _____

4. What happened to Lot's wife as they fled the burning cities of Sodom and Gomorrah? Why?

   _____

   _____

5. What is the Scripture reference for the Sacrifice of Isaac?

   _____

   _____

6. List the events studied to date in chronological order.

   _____

   _____

   _____

   _____

   _____

   _____

PLAGUES IN EGYPT
Worksheet

1. What is the approximate date of the Plagues in Egypt?

   _____

   _____

2. What is the Scripture reference for the Plagues in Egypt?

   _____

   _____

3. How did God speak to Moses? What did he tell him to do?

   _____

   _____

4. How many times did Moses appeal to Pharaoh to let the Israelites go?

   _____

   _____

5. What punishment did God send to the Egyptians because Pharaoh would not let the Israelites go?

   _____

   _____

6. What was the correlation between the plagues and Egyptian gods?

   _____

PLAGUES IN EGYPT
Project

Moses was raised up by God to be the leader of the Hebrews, and their deliverer from "the house of bondage." Pharaoh refused to let the people go, and plagues were sent upon Egypt to bring him into submission. Nine plagues had already visited the land; still Pharaoh's heart was hardened. One plague more, the tenth—terrible, fatal, effectual—was threatened before it came to happen. It was the death of all the first-born in Egypt, from the first-born of "the king upon his throne, to the first-born of the maidservant behind the mill." God, who knew the effect of this terrible stroke, directed that there should be a festival in commemoration of it, and that the Hebrews should stand ready for departure at the appointed time. The festival was called the Passover. The destroying angel would *pass over* the doors marked with the blood of a lamb which every Hebrew family was directed to slay, and eat in the posture of persons ready for a journey. This feast was afterwards observed by the Israelites to this day. Even now, once every year, they celebrate the Feast of the Passover, and tell of the wonderful deliverance of the Hebrews. This is an instance from which you see that our blessings should never be forgotten. The record of the Hebrews' remarkable deliverance has come down though the ages.

Pretend that you are a young Hebrew boy or girl and have just survived the plagues and the first Passover. Write a letter on the following page to a friend or grandparent describing what you have just been through.

Plagues in Egypt
Project, Page 2

Plagues in Egypt

1. Athor (corresponded to Aphrodite of the Greeks)
2. Ptah (pigmy or child)
3. Isis (wife of Osiris, goddess of maternity)
4. Osiris (god of the Nile, chief divinity of Egypt)
5. Neith (goddess of wisdom)
6. Bubastis (goddess of fire)
7. Apis (bull, god of nature)
8. Beg (hawk)
9. Ibis (crane)
10. Shau (cat)
11. Scarabaeus (beetle)

PLAGUES IN EGYPT
Teacher's Information

Ask the students what the Bible says about the worship of idols (refer to Exodus 20:1-6)?

When the Israelites sojourned in Egypt, they came in contact with more than forty-two deities, fifty local divinities and deified animals. The plagues which God inflicted on Pharaoh and the Egyptians for holding Israel in bondage, were specifically designed to show the utter impotency of their idols and idolatrous worship, and to reveal the might of JEHOVAH. Numbers 33:4 says, "For the Egyptians were burying all their firstborn, whom the Lord had killed among them. Also on their gods the Lord had executed judgements." The Nile and its fish were worshiped: "and all the waters that were in the river were turned to blood; and the fish that was in the river died; and the river stank." The frog was a sacred animal: "and the frogs came up and covered the land of Egypt," and they made everything loathsome. Entire cleanliness of the body was thought to be a religious obligation: "all the dust of the land became lice," so that all were defiled and could not enter their temples. These three plagues came by the delegated hand of Israel's High Priest. Beetles were everywhere sculptured and deified: "the land was corrupted by reason of the swarms of flies, "or the great Egyptian beetles. From the cattle of the fields was selected a type of the chief deity: "and all the cattle of Egypt died; but of the cattle of the children of Israel died not one." The fourth and fifth plagues came directly from the Lord. Ashes were a means of purification: "and Moses sprinkled it up toward Heaven; and it became a boil breaking forth with blains upon man, and upon beast" —the means of purification became a source of defilement. Nature's fruitfulness was symbolized by a god, each tree was a deity, and the best fruits were votive-offerings to idols: "and the hail smote throughout all the land of Egypt all that was in the field, both man and beast; and the hail smote every herb of the field, and brake every tree of the field." The wind was one of the deities: "and when it was morning the east wind brought the locusts; they covered the face of the whole earth, so the land was darkened; and they did eat every herb of the land, and all the fruit of the trees which the hail had left: and there remained not any green thing in the trees, or in the herbs of the field, through all the land of Egypt." The sun and darkness were each worshiped as gods: "and there was a thick darkness in all the land of Egypt for three days; they saw not one another, neither rose any from his place for three days; but all the children of Israel had light in their dwellings." These four plagues, foreshadowing the ultimate desolation and destruction to befall idolaters, came by the outstretched hand of the Prophet of Israel. The 10th plague was the execution of the final judgement: "and it came to pass, that at midnight the Lord smote all the first-born in the land of Egypt, from the first-born of Pharaoh that sat on his throne unto the first-born of the captive that was in the dungeon; and all the first-born of cattle." Justice was tempered with mercy: all the first-born unto Israel were sanctified— "therefore I sacrifice to the Lord all that openeth the matrix, being males; but all the first-born of my children I redeem." Exodus 7:12, 13:15.

PLAGUES IN EGYPT
Project 2

Draw a line from the plague to the corresponding deity.

 Nile changed to blood

 Khnum
controlled the Nile

 Frogs overran the land

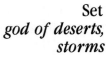 Set
god of deserts, storms

Gnats overran the land

Hathor
depicted with livestock head
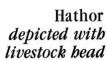

 Flies infest Egypt

Heqet
goddess of birth, depicted with the head of a frog

 Cattle found dead

Horus
god of the sun

 Boils infected the Egyptians

Nut
sky goddess

 Hail destroyed the crops

Re
symbolized by the fly

Locusts consumed the plants

Osiris
god of crops

 Darkness covered the land

Isis
goddess of healing

 Egyptian firstborn children died

Min
god of fertility

PLAGUES IN EGYPT

Project 2, Page 2

Answer key to previous page.

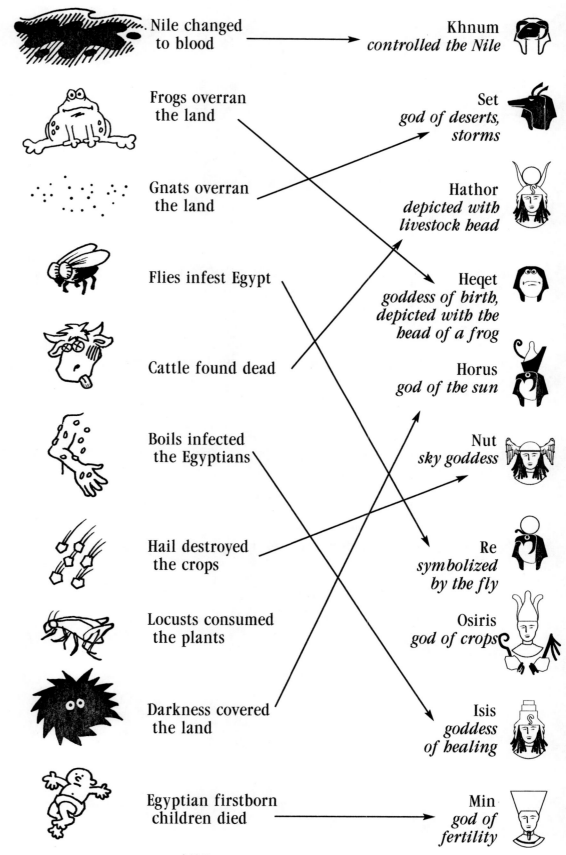

Nile changed to blood — Khnum *controlled the Nile*

Frogs overran the land

Gnats overran the land

Set *god of deserts, storms*

Hathor *depicted with livestock head*

Flies infest Egypt

Cattle found dead

Heqet *goddess of birth, depicted with the head of a frog*

Horus *god of the sun*

Boils infected the Egyptians

Nut *sky goddess*

Hail destroyed the crops

Re *symbolized by the fly*

Locusts consumed the plants

Osiris *god of crops*

Darkness covered the land

Isis *goddess of healing*

Egyptian firstborn children died — Min *god of fertility*

PLAGUES IN EGYPT
Test

1. What is the scripture reference for the plagues in Egypt?

   _____

   _____

2. What is the approximate date of the plagues in Egypt?

   _____

   _____

3. Why did God speak to Moses through a burning bush?

   _____

   _____

4. How many times did Moses make an appeal to Pharaoh?

   _____

   _____

5. When Pharaoh refused to listen to what Moses said how did God punish the Egyptians?

   _____

   _____

6. What was the relationship between the plagues and Egyptian gods?

   _____

   _____

   _____

   _____

   _____

Plagues in Egypt
Test, Page 2

Review

1. What did God do on the seventh day of Creation?

   _____

   _____

2. Why was God pleased with Abel's offering and not Cain's?

   _____

   _____

3. What was the name of the son born to Abraham and Sarah?

   _____

   _____

4. What did Joseph dream about his family at the age of seventeen?

   _____

   _____

5. To what was Jacob's name changed? Why?

   _____

   _____

6. Who was the first woman Pharaoh?

   _____

   _____

7. On the back of this page list all events covered in chronological order.

THE EXODUS
Worksheet

1. What is the approximate date of the Exodus?

   _____

   _____

2. What is the Scripture reference for the Exodus?

   _____

   _____

3. What was the tenth plague?

   _____

   _____

4. How were the Israelites spared from the tenth plague?

   _____

   _____

5. What did God tell the Israelites to do?

   _____

   _____

6. When Pharaoh tried to recapture the
   Israelites and put them back into
   slavery, what did God do?

   _____

   _____

   _____

   _____

   _____

   _____

THE EXODUS
Project

Read Exodus 14.

Using complete sentences, write a paragraph describing the Biblical meaning in the picture.

_____

_____

_____

_____

_____

_____

_____

_____

_____

Moses

P R E S E N T E D   B Y

THE EXODUS
Project, Page 2

Moses, a Play

Narrator: The Israelites in Egypt during the captivity became strong and numerous. Pharaoh feared they would take over Egypt and ordered all male Israelite boys to be slaughtered at birth. Moses mother attempted to hide him by placing him in a reed basket and putting the basket among the reeds in the Nile River. Pharaoh's daughter found Moses in the Nile and was compassionate toward him. She took him home and raised him as her own. He was raised as an Egyptian, but he never forgot that he was one of the children of Israel. The Pharaoh had no knowledge of Joseph and how helpful the Israelites had been for so long in the past.

Scene One

(Scene one begins with an Egyptian taskmaster and slave. Moses watches from the side of stage as the taskmaster strikes the slave.)

Egyptian Taskmaster: (With whip in hand) Work harder! You must make more bricks. We are falling behind and Pharaoh expects us to produce more. (Strike the slave.)
Moses: Why are you beating the Hebrew slave? He is working as hard as he can.
Egyptian Taskmaster: He is only a slave, Pharaoh's property. He is a Hebrew, they must be treated this way or they may attempt to rebel against us.
Moses: Would you treat me this way? I am a Hebrew. Had I not been raised with Pharaoh you would be treating me this way also.
Egyptian Taskmaster: Work! Work! (Striking him with the whip—slave cries out in pain.)
Moses: (Looks to see if others are watching and picks up a large rock and strikes the Egyptian Overseer killing him.) He says angrily while beating him with the rock "You must stop!"
Egyptian Overseer: (Sighs in pain. Falls to the ground dead.)
Moses: What have I done? I have killed him. I must bury him quickly. (Pull the body to the side and pretend to dig a hole in the sand. Have some large rocks made out of cardboard or styrofoam to pull him behind.) Pharaoh must not know.

Scene Two

Narrator: Moses thought all night about what he had done. The following day he went back out to see the Hebrew slaves. While he was there he encountered two Hebrew slaves fighting with each other. (Open with two Hebrews striking one another.)
Moses: Why are you beating up your brother?
Slave One: Who made you a prince and a judge over us?
Moses: I am only trying to stop you from harming each other. We have enough oppression from the Egyptians without fighting with one another.
Slave Two: Do you intend to kill me as you killed the Egyptian?
Moses: (Showing fear on his face says to the slave): How did you know about that? (Then says to himself): Surely, this thing is known. If Pharaoh hears of this he will have me killed. I must flee.

Scene Three

Narrator: Moses fled from Egypt and dwelt in the land of Midian. One day he decided to rest and sat down at a well to get a drink.
Moses: I need to rest. I have been walking all day. A drink will cool me down. (Enter Zipporah and her sisters.)

THE EXODUS
Project

Zipporah: (Looks at her sisters.)
We must draw water from the well to water father's flock.

Sister One: Very soon we will have the troughs filled and we can water the sheep.

Shepherd One: Move away from here. We cannot wait for your sheep to drink, we are in a hurry.

Shepherd Two: Move along we must water our flock! Away with you.

Zipporah: Please! We have worked hard to fill the troughs. We will be finished and then you may use the well.

Shepherd One: Get out of our way!

Moses: What is the matter? The women were here before you. Don't treat them this way. (Moses picks up a pail of water and helps the women. Shepherds move off to the side.) Let them water their flocks.

Shepherd Two: (Looking at shepherd one.) Let's wait instead of causing trouble. It won't take long. (Then under his breath he says): We should not have to wait on these women.

Zipporah: (Looking at Moses) We can never repay you for what you have done. Please accept our thanks.

Scene Four
(Moses is sitting next to the well and Zipporah enters.)

Moses: Why have you come back so soon? Did you leave a watering jug?

Zipporah: We told our father how you helped us today and he would like you to come home with us for dinner.

Moses: I would like to meet your father.

Zipporah: Follow me.
(Moses, Zipporah and sisters walk to one side of the stage.)

Moses: Is that your father I see in the distance?

Jethro: (Walk in up center aisle from the back.) Zipporah, is this the man who helped you today?

Zipporah: Yes, Father, this is Moses.

Jethro: Let us feast. You have shown kindness to my family and I want us to break bread.

Moses: That would please me. (Jethro, Moses, Zipporah and sisters sit down to eat.)

Scene Five

Narrator: Jethro was so pleased with Moses that eventually he gave Zipporah to him in marriage. Moses tended flocks for his father-in-law and had a son.
(Moses in the field tending sheep.)

Moses: Move! (Looking at flock.)
We must keep moving. We are almost to Horeb. Now, you may rest and graze. (Moses sits down to watch the flock. Use party streamers attached to a cardboard rock and blow from underneath with a fan. Flames of fire burst forth from a bush.)

Moses: Gasp!!!

God from the Bush: (Crackle sound... use a recording)

Moses: I will now turn aside and see this great sight. Why is the bush not consumed by the fire?

God from the Bush: (Have someone read from off stage the parts of the burning bush.) Moses, Moses!

Moses: Here I am.

God from the Bush: Do not come any closer to this place. Take your sandals off your feet, for the place where you stand is holy ground. I am the God of your Father—the God of Abraham, the God of Isaac, and the God of Jacob.

Moses: (Falls down and hide face.)
I must hide my face.

God from the Bush: I have surely seen the oppression of My people who are in Egypt, and have heard their cry because of their taskmasters, for I know their sorrows. So I

THE EXODUS
Project

have come down to deliver them out of the hand of the Egyptians, and to bring them up from that land and to a land flowing with milk and honey, to the place of the Hittites and Amorites and the Perrizzites and the Hivites and the Jebusites. Come now, therefore, and I will send you to Pharaoh that you may bring my people, the children of Israel out of Egypt.

Moses: Who am I that I should go to Pharaoh, and that I should bring the children of Israel out of Egypt?

God from the Bush: I will certainly be with you. And this shall be a sign to you: When you have brought the people out of Egypt you shall serve God on this mountain.

Moses: Indeed, when I come to the children of Israel and say the God of your Fathers has sent me to you, and they say to me, "What is His name?" What shall I say to them?

God from the Bush: You shall say to the children of Israel I AM WHO I AM has sent me to you. The Lord God of your fathers, the God of Abraham, the God of Isaac, and the God of Jacob has sent me to you. This is my name forever, and this is my memorial to all generations. I will bring you out of the afflictions of Egypt. Say to Pharaoh: The Lord God of the Hebrews has met with us. Please let us go three days journey into the wilderness, that we may sacrifice to the Lord our God.

Moses: What if Pharaoh will not let us go?

God from the Bush: I am sure that he will not let you go, so I will stretch out my hand and strike Egypt with all my wonders and after that he will let you go.

Moses: What if they will not believe me?

God from the Bush: What is that in your hand?

Moses: A rod.

God from the Bush: Cast it onto the ground.

Moses: (When the rod hits the ground it becomes a serpent.) A serpent! NOooo!!!!! (Moses flees.)

God from the Bush: Reach out and take it by the tail that they may believe that the Lord God of their Fathers has appeared to you. (Moses reaches to pick up the snake and it becomes a rod again. Scene ends with lights dimming and Moses saying the following.)

Moses: But, Lord, I am so slow of speech that they may not believe me.

Narrator: The Lord God gave Moses other signs to convince the people of who He was. But, Moses was fearful that he could not communicate well. So the Lord agreed to send Aaron, Moses' brother with him. As the Lord foretold, Pharaoh did refuse to let the Israelites go into the wilderness when Moses asked. Moses and Aaron pleaded with Pharaoh, but his heart was hard. God sent plagues to punish the Egyptians. After the tenth and final plague, the death of the first born, Pharaoh relented and not only allowed the Israelites to leave but gave them much to get them to leave quickly. Shortly after they left, Pharaoh changed his mind and took his army after them to bring them back. The Israelites were ushered through the Red Sea on dry land when God parted the water for them and caused the parted water to come crashing down on the Egyptians when they attempted to follow in pursuit. God had faithfully delivered His people from the Egyptian oppression as He promised.

The End

THE EXODUS
Project

Moses, a Play (Page 7)

1. Use a piece of 45" fabric. A plainer piece of fabric should be used for the Hebrew outfit as they were slaves and dressed more simply. In scenes one and two, Moses should have stripes and jewels as he was part of Pharaoh's household. Measure from the shoulder to just below the knee to determine the amount of fabric needed (Approx. 2 yds). Old sheets may be used, too.

2. Fold a two yard length in half as shown on left.

3. Fold 45" width in half as shown on left.

4. Cut out neck hole in the corner with two folds as shown on left. (It's easier to cut a second time than to cut too much the first time.)

5. Cut belt from different colored fabric as shown on left. (Approx. 1.5 yards long) Fringe the edge with scissors.

6. Tie belt around waist.

7. Cut fabric for head piece in one yard squares and cut head band one yard long by one and one half inches wide. Allow children to decorate headbands with markers or fabric paint.

8. Have children wear sandals for shoes.

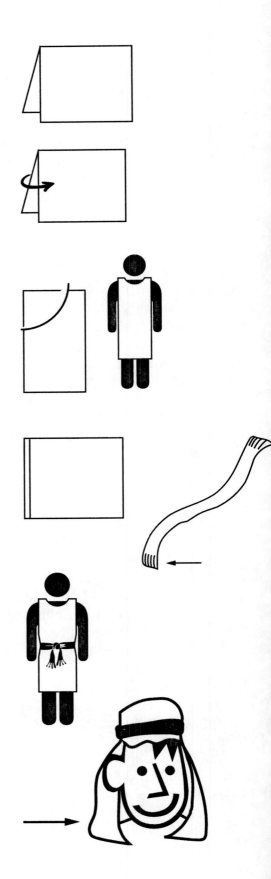

THE EXODUS
Test

1. What is the approximate date of the Exodus?

   _____

   _____

2. What is the Scripture reference for the Exodus?

   _____

   _____

3. What was the tenth plague?

   _____

   _____

4. What does the "Passover" symbolize?

   _____

   _____

5. How did God save the Israelites from being taken captive by Pharaoh again?

   _____

   _____

Review

1. How did man fall out of fellowship with God?

   _____

   _____

2. What is the Scripture reference for the story of Cain and Abel?

   _____

   _____

3. What did God tell Noah to take in the ark?

   _____

4. What occurred during the First Intermediate Period in Egypt?

_____

_____

5. What are hieroglyphics?

_____

_____

6. Who was Potiphar?

_____

_____

7. How many tribes of Israel were there? Name them.

_____

_____

8. For what is Hammurabi known?

_____

_____

9. Why did Moses' mother place him in a basket as an infant and put the basket in the reeds by the Nile River?

_____

_____

10. On the back of this page list all events covered in chronological order.

TEN COMMANDMENTS
Worksheet

1. What is the Scripture reference for the Ten Commandments?

   _____

   _____

2. What is the approximate date of the Ten Commandments?

   _____

   _____

3. To whom did God give the Ten Commandments? Where did He do this?

   _____

   _____

4. What purpose do the Ten Commandment serve?

   _____

   _____

5. Write down each of the Ten Commandments in order.

   _____

   _____

   _____

   _____

   _____

   _____

   _____

   _____

   _____

   _____

TEN COMMANDMENTS
Project

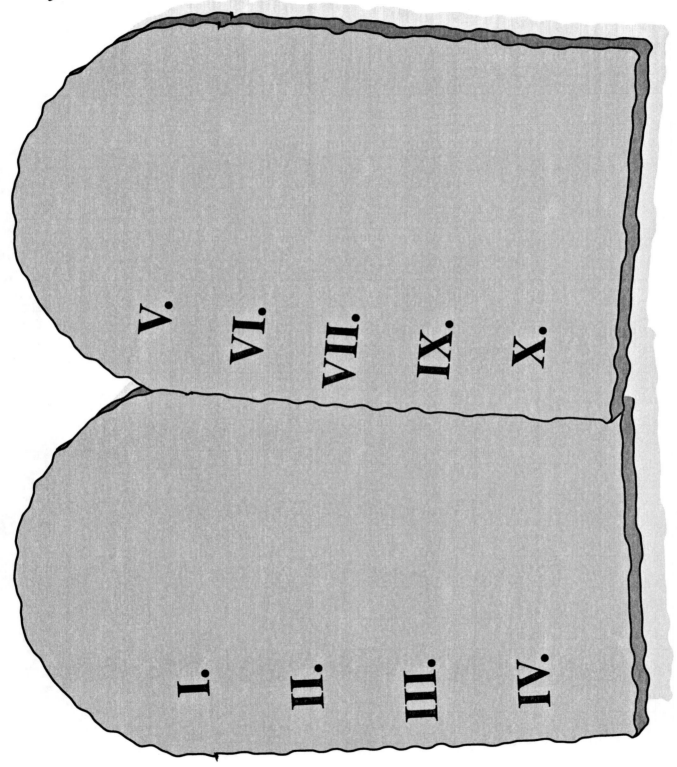

Write down each of the Ten Commandments next to the appropriate number.

Ten Commandments
Test

1. Where did God reveal the Ten Commandments to Moses?

   _____

   _____

2. Write down each of the Ten Commandments in order.

   _____

   _____

   _____

   _____

   _____

   _____

   _____

   _____

   _____

   _____

3. Where can the Ten Commandments be found in Scripture?

   _____

   _____

Review

1. On the back write down all the events learned to date in chronological order. Include dates for cards number 8, 12 and 24 and Scripture references where applicable for all events.

AMENHOTEP IV AND MONOTHEISM
Worksheet

1. What is the approximate date of Amenhotep IV and monotheism?

   _____

   _____

2. During what dynasty did Amenhotep IV rule?

   _____

   _____

3. Which god did Amenhotep IV declare as the only god?

   _____

   _____

4. What is monotheism?

   _____

   _____

5. Why did Amenhotep change his name to Akhnaton?

   _____

   _____

6. Who was Tiy?

   _____

   _____

7. What was Tutankhamon relationship to Amenhotep IV?

   _____

   _____

Nefertiti (on the left), Akhnaton

AMENHOTEP AND MONOTHEISM
Project

Amenhotep and his queen Nefertiti playing "senet".   The most controversial figure in Egyptian history, Amenhotep IV (reigned 1361 - 1344 BC) changed his name to Akhnaton after transferring his worship from the many national gods, headed by Amon-Re, to Aton, the solar disk, in a nearly exclusive cult. The stiff resistance to his intention of converting the whole country led to his creation of a new capital city far from Thebes, in an area of present-day Tell el-Amarna. The art that he commissioned was unlike that of any other reign, showing the royal family in many nonceremonial activities. The noble hymns composed to Aton may have influenced the Psalms of David.

Color this picture.

AMENHOTEP IV AND MONOTHEISM
Test

1. What is the approximate date of Amenhotep IV?

   _____

   _____

2. Who was the wife of Amenhotep IV?

   _____

   _____

3. Why did Amenhotep IV decree Aton to be the only god?

   _____

   _____

4. Who was Amenhotep IV's half brother?

   _____

   _____

Review

1. What did God create on the fifth day of Creation?

   _____

   _____

2. What is the Scripture reference for the Fall in the Garden?

   _____

   _____

3. What is the Scripture reference for the Tower of Babel?

   _____

   _____

4. Who was the first person to unify Upper and Lower Egypt?

   _____

   _____

5. What was the name of Abraham's wife?

   _____

   _____

6. What was the name of the one righteous man that God found living in Sodom and Gomorrah?

   _____

   _____

7. List all the events learned to date in chronological order (continue on back).

   _____

   _____

   _____

   _____

   _____

   _____

   _____

   _____

   _____

   _____

   _____

   _____

   _____

REIGN OF TUTANKHAMON
Worksheet

1. What is the approximate date of the Reign of Tutankhamon?

    _____

    _____

2. What was one of the largest archeological finds made on November 4th, 1922?
    Who made this discovery?

    _____

    _____

3. How old was Tutankhamon when he ascended the throne?

    _____

    _____

4. Who were Tutankhamon's grandfather and father?

    _____

    _____

5. How old was Tutankhamon when he died?

    _____

    _____

6. Why was Tutankhamon's name changed during his life?

    _____

    _____

7. Why was the discovery of Tutankhamon's tomb so important?

    _____

    _____

    _____

REIGN OF TUTANKHAMON
Project—Literature Unit

Tut's Mummy Lost...and Found by Judy Donnelly

CHAPTER ONE: The King is Dead

1. How old was Tutankhamon when he died?

   _____

2. What is the Land of the Dead? Describe it.

   _____

   _____

3. What did the Egyptians believe they needed to take with them to the Land of the Dead?

   _____

   _____

4. What was the purpose of mummies?

   _____

   _____

5. How many days did it take to make a mummy?

   _____

   _____

6. Where was Tutankhamon buried? Why?

   _____

   _____

7. On the back of this page draw a picture of Tutankhamon's funeral parade.

8. The priest would touch the mouth, eyes and ears on the mummy. Why did they do this?

   _____

   _____

9. What does the Bible say about the Egyptians view of death? (Matthew 6:19-21, John 14:1-6)

   _____

   _____

REIGN OF TUTANKHAMON
Project—Literature Unit

Tut's Mummy Lost...and Found by Judy Donnelly

CHAPTER TWO: The Lost King

1. What is an archaeologist?

_____

_____

2. What did archaeologists find in Egypt in the 1800's?

_____

_____

3. What was the Valley of the Kings? What were they hoping to find in the Valley of the Kings?

_____

_____

4. Who was the one archaeologist that never gave up looking for lost tombs?

_____

_____

CHAPTER THREE: The Search

1. Howard Carter believed he would find Tutankhamon's tomb.

   Who did he get to finance his expedition?

_____

_____

2. What were the conditions in which Carter and his men worked?

_____

_____

_____

REIGN OF TUTANKHAMON
Project—Literature Unit

Tut's Mummy Lost...and Found by Judy Donnelly

3. After five years and no significant finds Lord Carnarvon was ready to give up. What was Carter's response?

_____

_____

4. In November, 1922 Carter and his men began digging again. What happened on the third day of the dig?

_____

_____

5. For whom did Carter send?

_____

_____

CHAPTER FOUR: The Discover

1. What did Carter see as he looked in the hole in the door of the tomb?

_____

_____

2. What did the air smell like that escaped from the tomb?

_____

_____

3. Why was Howard Carter so excited? What did he see all around him?

_____

_____

_____

REIGN OF TUTANKHAMON
Project—Literature Unit

Tut's Mummy Lost...and Found by Judy Donnelly

CHAPTER FIVE: The King is Dead

1. Why did the discovery of Tutankhamon's tomb make headlines all over the world?

   _____

   _____

2. What name did newspapers give to Pharaoh Tutankhamon?

   _____

   _____

3. After months of clearing away hundreds of treasures Howard Carter was finally ready to open the sealed door. What did he find behind it?

   _____

   _____

4. What happened to Lord Carnarvon? What did the newspaper say about him? Why?

   _____

   _____

   _____

   _____

REIGN OF TUTANKHAMON
Project—Literature Unit

Tut's Mummy Lost...and Found by Judy Donnelly

Answers

CHAPTER ONE
1. Eighteen
2. The Land of the Dead is where the Egyptian's believe one's spirit travels upon death.

   There the dead person will do all the things they loved to do when they were alive. It is a place of perpetual happiness.
3. They needed to take food, furniture, clothing, jewelry and games. Anything they used in their earthly life. Most of all you need your body.
4. The spirit cannot move on without out its body. Mummies were made to dry out bodies so they would last forever.
5. Seventy days.
6. In a secret underground tomb, where grave robbers cannot break in and steal all the treasures or disturb the body.
7. Look on page 10 and 11 for examples.
8. To enable the mummy's spirit to speak, see and hear.
9. The Egyptians put their faith in earthly treasure, spending their lives storing up for their death. The Bible tells us that the opposite is true. All our earthly treasures will rot and decay, but our faith in God never will.

CHAPTER TWO
1. Scientists who dig in the earth to find clues to the past.
2. Temples, wall paintings, statues of animals, gods and mummies.
3. A valley where many tombs were discovered. They hoped to find Tutankhamon.
4. Howard Carter

CHAPTER THREE
1. Lord Carnarvon
2. Terrible. It is rocky, burning, dry, hot and dusty.
3. Carter begged Carnarvon for one more try.
4. They find a step and then another, until they see a whole stairway leading to a secret door.
5. Lord Carnarvon who is in England.

CHAPTER FOUR
1. Incredible sights! Golden chariots, jeweled chests, couches in the shapes of animals, vases, and statues. Everything glitters with gold!
2. Sweet from ancient funeral flowers.
3. Treasure, specifically two statues of the king, big as life and Tutankhamon's golden throne.

CHAPTER FIVE
1. It was the greatest treasure ever found.
2. King Tut
3. A huge golden cabinet. Inside the cabinet is a great stone box. And in the box are three coffins nested one inside the other.
4. He died from a bad insect bite. The new papers say it is a mummy's curse. They say Tut is mad because his tomb was opened.

REIGN OF TUTANKHAMON

Project 2

1. Copy one pattern per student on to card stock.
2. Have students cut out the mask.
3. Attach tin foil to both pieces of mask. (Spray glue works best.)
4. Spray paint both pieces gold. (If you use gold foil in 3 above, this step is not necessary.)
5. Have students score the lines of King Tut's face mask and collar with a pencil on the foil by using various pictures in books. (One of the best is *Tut's Mummy Lost... and Found,* page 44.)
6. Paint the face mask and collar with acrylic paint. Construction paper may also be used for the "collar" of the mask.
7. Spray the mask with clear spray paint to seal it.
8. Glue the mask to the collar. (A hot glue gun is recommended.)
   You may want to glue the completed mask to foamboard.

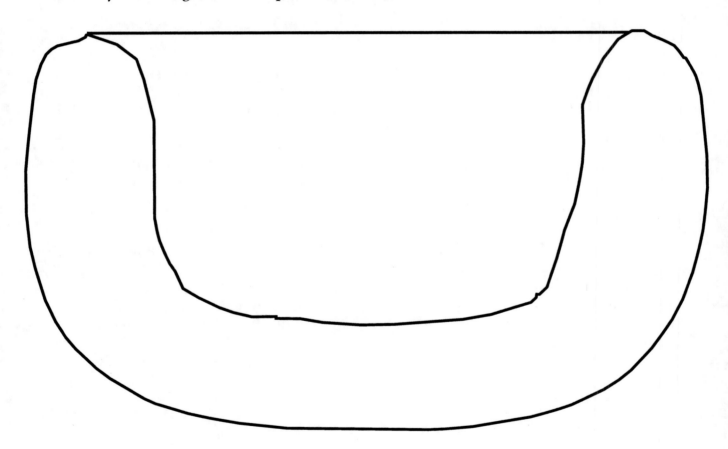

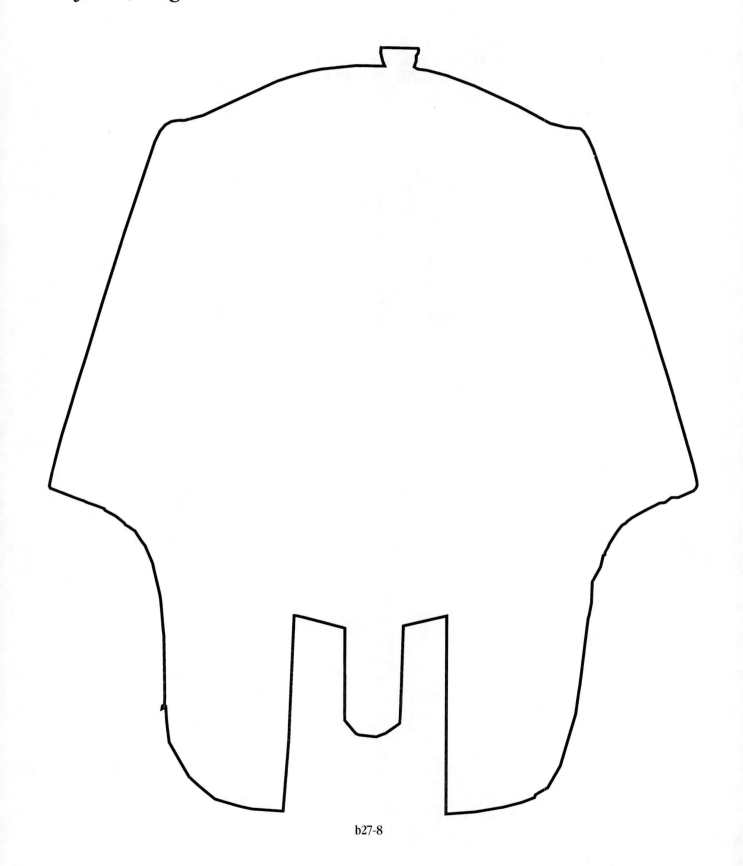

REIGN OF TUTANKHAMON
Project 3

View *King Tut, Tomb of Treasure.* Experience the wonder and mystery of King Tutankhamon's tomb. Visit the actual tomb, the Cairo Museum, and the New Orleans Museum of Art for a glimpse at the magnificent artifacts that were buried with Tut.

The video was produced by Public Media Video.

REIGN OF TUTANKHAMON
Test

1. What is the approximate date of the Reign of Tutankhamon?

   _____

   _____

2. What discovery did Howard Carter make?

   _____

   _____

3. How old was Tutankhamon when he ascended the throne?

   _____

   _____

4. How long did Tutankhamon reign?

   _____

   _____

5. Why did Tutankhamon change his name?

   _____

   _____

6. Why was the finding of Tutankhamon's tomb such an important archeological discovery?

   _____

   _____

Review

1. What covenant did God establish with Noah?

   _____

   _____

   _____

REIGN OF TUTANKHAMON
Test, Page 2

2. What occurred during the Old Kingdom in Egypt?

_____

_____

3. What is the Scripture reference for God's Covenant with Abraham?

_____

4. How did God test Abraham's faith?

_____

_____

5. Name the twelve tribes of Israel.

_____   _____

_____   _____

_____   _____

_____   _____

_____   _____

_____   _____

6. Who was Hammurabi?

_____

_____

7. How did the Hyksos take Egypt by surprise?

_____

_____

8. Where was Moses raised?

_____

_____

9. On the back list the events covered to date in chronological order.

LATER NEW KINGDOM
Worksheet

1. What is the approximate date of the Later New Kingdom?

   _____

   _____

2. What gains were made during the Later New Kingdom?

   _____

   _____

3. Who was the first Pharaoh of the 19th dynasty?

   _____

   _____

4. Place the following names in the order of father, son, grandson.

   Seti   Ramses II   Ramses I

   _____

   _____

5. What is the most depicted event in Egyptian history?

   _____

   _____

6. What is Ramses II known for building?

   _____

   _____

LATER NEW KINGDOM
Project

Read the section entitled "Visit to a Temple" in the *Time Traveller Book of Pharaohs and Pyramids.* Using complete sentences to compare the Egyptian view of worship to a Hebrew/Biblical view of worship.

_____

_____

_____

_____

_____

_____

_____

_____

_____

_____

_____

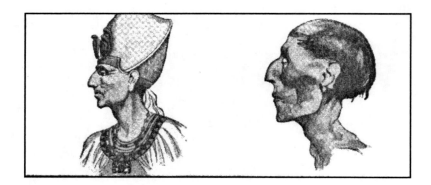

LATER NEW KINGDOM
Project 2

View the 60 minute video entitled *Egypt: Quest for Eternity* produced by National Geographic Video Classics with your students. This exceptional video will help in understanding the Egyptian culture.

Join Egyptologists as they unravel and interpret the riddles of Egypt's intriguing past.

LATER NEW KINGDOM IN EGYPT
Test

1. What is the approximate date of the Later New Kingdom in Egypt?

   _____

   _____

2. What gains did Egypt make during this period?

   _____

   _____

3. To which dynasty does Ramses I belong?

   _____

   _____

4. What is the most depicted event in Egyptian history?

   _____

   _____

5. Who led Egypt in the Battle of Kadsh?

   _____

   _____

Review

1. On the back list the twelve tribes of Israel.

2. On the back list the Ten Commandments. Where can the Ten Commandments
   be found in Scripture?

   _____

3. On the back list all the events covered to date in chronological order.

DAVIDIC KINGDOM
Worksheet

1. What is the Scripture reference for the Davidic Kingdom?

   _____

   _____

2. What are the approximate dates of the Davidic KIngdom?

   _____

   _____

3. With God's direction where did the prophet Samuel visit to find the next king of Israel?

   _____

   _____

4. Who was selected as Israel's next king?

   _____

   _____

5. Who did David defeat?

   _____

   _____

6. Why did King Saul become jealous of David?

   _____

   _____

7. What did King Saul attempt to do to David?

   _____

   _____

8. How long was David's reign over Israel?

   _____

   _____

DAVIDIC KINGDOM
Project

After reading about David in I & II Samuel and I Chronicles choose four favorite events and illustrate them in the frames below.

DAVIDIC KINGDOM
Project 2

Read I Samuel 16.

Using complete sentences, write a paragraph describing the Biblical meaning in the picture.

_____

_____

_____

_____

_____

_____

_____

_____

_____

_____

DAVIDIC KINGDOM
Test

1. Where in Scripture can we find the Davidic Kingdom?

   _____

   _____

2. What are the approximate dates of the Davidic Kingdom?

   _____

   _____

3. At the direction of God who did Samuel chose to be the next king of Israel?

   _____

   _____

4. Why did King Saul become jealous of David?

   _____

   _____

5. Who was Goliath?

   _____

   _____

6. Approximately how many years did Solomon reign as king of Israel?

   _____

   _____

DAVIDIC KINGDOM
Test

Review

1. When God decided to flood the earth who was the one man who found favor in God's sight?

   _____

   _____

2. What do some archeologists believe may be the ruins of the Tower of Babel?

   _____

   _____

3. What was the purpose of the pyramids?

   _____

   _____

4. Where in Scripture can we find the Call of Abram?

   _____

5. What major advances occurred during the Middle Kingdom in Egypt?

   _____

   _____

6. When Pharaoh found out that Joseph's brothers had come to see him, what did he do?

   _____

   _____

7. Who may have been the princess that pulled Moses from the Nile River?

   _____

   _____

8. What is the fifth commandment?

   _____

9. On the back list all the events covered to date in chronological order.

SOLOMON'S REIGN
Worksheet

1. What is the Scripture reference for the Reign of Solomon?

   _____

   _____

2. What are the approximate dates of the Reign of Solomon?

   _____

   _____

3. After David died who became king?

   _____

   _____

4. In a dream God asked King Solomon, "What shall I give you?" For what did Solomon ask?

   _____

   _____

5. What plan of his father's was Solomon able to carry out?

   _____

   _____

6. What famous queen came to seek out Solomon's wisdom?

   _____

7. What happened to Solomon's relationship with God before he died?

   _____

   _____

Solomon's Reign
Project

Building the Temple

TEMPLE OF SOLOMON.

With the instructions below turn your classroom (or a room at home) into a replica of Solomon's Temple. Talk to the children about how many years went into the planning and building of the Temple. Read I Kings 6 - 8 and possibly The Victor Journey Through the Bible , pages 132 - 133, and The Kregel Pictorial Guide to The Temple.
After reading this let the students come up with ideas for turning your class into the temple. It is also a good idea to see if a local pastor or someone with knowledge of the temple can come in upon completion and discuss the symbolism with the children.
Below are some ideas for implementing this. They are in no way complete. Be creative and have fun. You should allow one Friday afternoon for this project and speaker. It also helps to have a couple extra moms to help (or to work with other homeschool families).

1. Hang brown bulletin board paper on a few of the walls to represent the cedarwood.
   Draw on the paper flowers, cherubim, and palm trees to represent those carved in
   the wood.
2. At the front of the room make the inner sanctuary. Hang yellow bulletin board paper to
   represent the gold overlay. (Gold foil is both better and more expensive.)
3. Put a desk in the outer sanctuary to represent the altar and cover it with yellow paper.
   Cover another desk with yellow paper to use as the table of gold on which the show
   bread was kept.
4. Make two cherubim by drawing, painting, and cutting them from refrigerator boxes.
   Put them in the inner sanctuary.
5. Using another refrigerator, make a door for the inner sanctuary. Use desks or other
   furniture items to separate the inner sanctuary from the outer.
6. Make lampstands from cardboard (or borrow from a party rental store).
   Place the lampstands in the front of the inner sanctuary.
7. Have students bring in bowls, ladles, etc. and cover them with gold foil for use in the
   temple.
8. Make the ark of the covenant from a box and cover it with yellow paper. Attach two
   dowels/rods to the sides with which to "carry" it. Place the Ten Commandments inside
   it. (Remember card #25 project?) Make two more cheribum and place on the top facing
   each other. Place the ark in the inner sanctuary.

This is not intended to be an exact replica. The more resources you have the more elaborate you may want to be. The ultimate idea is to teach children about the extraordinary symbolism and work that went into building a temple by God's design.

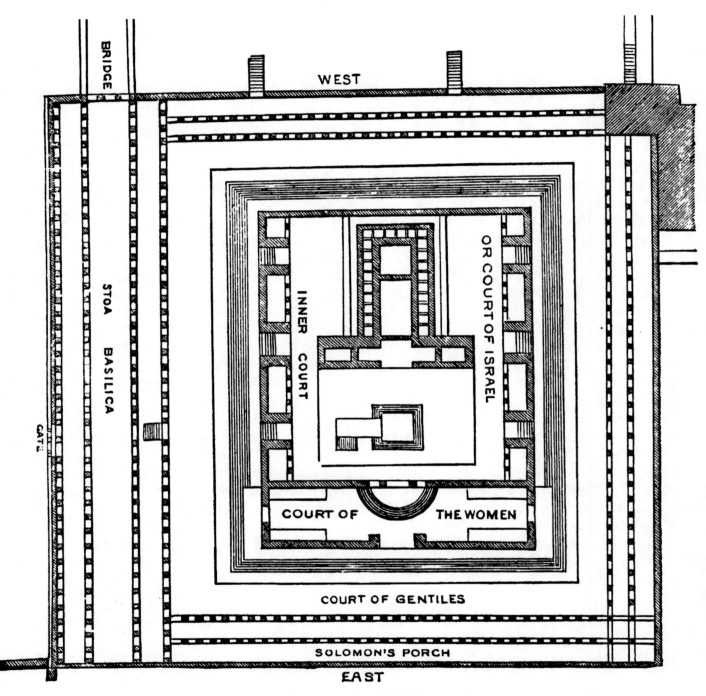

DIAGRAM OF TEMPLE.

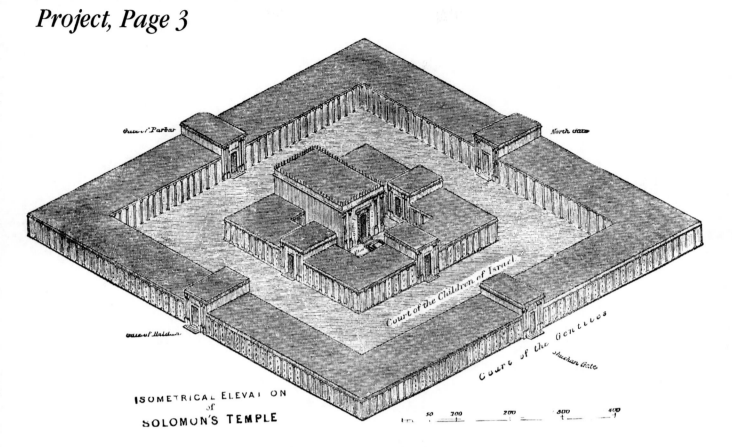

ISOMETRICAL ELEVATION
of
SOLOMON'S TEMPLE

SOLOMON'S REIGN

Test

1. What are the approximate dates of Solomon's Reign?

   _____

   _____

2. What is the Scripture reference for Solomon's Reign?

   _____

   _____

3. Who succeeded David as King?

   _____

   _____

4. What request did Solomon make of God?

   _____

   _____

5. In the later years of Solomon's life what happened with his relationship to God?

   _____

   _____

6. Who succeeded Solomon as King?

   _____

   _____

Review

1. On the back list all events covered to date in chronological order. Place Scripture references at the appropriate events. List dates for events numbered 9, 14 and 24.

ALEXANDER THE GREAT CONQUERS EGYPT
Worksheet

1. What is the approximate date of Alexander's conquering Egypt?

   _____

   _____

2. In 525 B.C. which Persian ruler conquered Egypt? What did this ruler not approve of?

   _____

   _____

3. Who conquered the entire Persian empire including Egypt?

   _____

   _____

4. Why was Alexander welcomed by the Egyptians?

   _____

   _____

5. What did Alexander tell his generals about who should succeed him upon his death?

   _____

   _____

6. Who was Ptolemy I?

   _____

   _____

   _____

   _____

ALEXANDER THE GREAT CONQUERS EGYPT
Project

Alexander the Great triumphant.

Dynasties 28 - 30 represented a last flickering of relative independence for Egypt before Persia took over again (Dynasty 31, the last numbered one). When Persia finally lost Egypt, it had lost almost everything: Alexander the Great (lived 356 - 323 B.C.), the world-conqueror from Macedonia, "delivered" Egypt in 332 B.C., only months before his decisive victory over the Persian Empire in Mesopotamia. Crowned as pharoah at Memphis, Alexander found the city of Alexandria at the western end of the Delta. This was destined to become one of the greatest cities of the world. After Alexander's death, his vast empire was divided among his leading generals, who launched new dynasties. The line founded by his general Ptolemy, who became pharoah in 305, was to last until 30 B.C.

Color this.

ALEXANDER THE GREAT CONQUERS EGYPT
Test

1. What is the approximate date of Alexander conquering Egypt?

   _____

2. Who was Cambyses?

   _____

   _____

3. When Alexander conquered Egypt why was he so welcomed by the Egyptian people?

   _____

   _____

4. Who came to rule over Egypt after Alexander's death?

   _____

   _____

Review

1. What is the Scripture reference for Creation?

   _____

2. Why did God curse Cain?

   _____

   _____

3. What is another name for Menes?

   _____

   _____

4. What did God covenant with Abraham?

   _____

   _____

5. Why did God destroy Sodom and Gomorrah?

_____

_____

6. Why did Joseph's brothers sell him into slavery?

_____

_____

7. What did Joseph do to secure food for Egypt during the famine?

_____

_____

8. What was each plague in Egypt a direct attack on?

_____

_____

9. What was the Exodus?

_____

_____

10. On the back list all the event covered to date in chronological; order.

EGYPT FALLS TO ROME
Worksheet

1. What is the approximate date when Egypt fell to Rome?

   _____

   _____

2. What Roman general supported Cleopatra during the Civil War in 48 BC?

   _____

   _____

3. Who murdered Julius Caesar? Why?

   _____

   _____

4. Who ruled the Roman Empire after Julius Caesar died?

   _____

   _____

5. Who did Cleopatra marry?

   _____

   _____

6. Why did Anthony and Cleopatra kill themselves?

   _____

   _____

7. To what did Octavius change his name?

   _____

   _____

8. What happened to the Egyptian people during the rule of Octavius?

   _____

   _____

   _____

EGYPT FALLS TO ROME
Project

Caesar and Cleopatra

Julius Caesar, arriving in Egypt in 48 B.C. in pursuit of Pompeii, his rival for supremacy in Rome, fell in love with Cleopatra VII and supported her disputed claim to the throne. After his assassination in 44 B.C., a new contender for Roman leadership, Mark Antony, became Cleopatra's new champion. They jointly ruled Egypt and large parts of the Near East until defeated by Augustus (Octavius), soon to become the first Roman emperor. Antony and Cleopatra committed suicide in 30 B.C., and Egypt became the province of the Roman Empire, supplying Rome with much of its grain. When the Empire split in two, in 395 A.D., Egypt found itself in the eastern, Byzantine, half. One of the great centers of early Christianity, Egypt was the original home of monasticism. The so-called Coptic art of this period is highly regarded today. Conquered by the Arabs in the 640's, Egypt has been Islamic ever since.

EGYPT FALLS TO ROME
Test

1. What is the approximate date of Egypt's fall to Rome?

   _____

2. Who was Julius Caesar?

   _____

   _____

3. Who murdered Julius Caesar? Why?

   _____

   _____

4. Who was Octavius? What did he conquer?

   _____

   _____

5. Why did Antony and Cleopatra commit suicide?

   _____

   _____

6. To what did Octavius change his name?

   _____

Review

1. Why did God cause people to speak many new languages at the time of the time of the
   Tower of Babel?

   _____

   _____

2. What is the age when pyramids were built known as?

   _____

   _____

3. What is the Scripture reference for the Call of Abram?

   _____

   _____

4. What did God ask Abraham to do to Isaac?

   _____

   _____

5. What did Joseph do for Pharaoh while in prison that resulted in Pharaoh putting Joseph second in command of all Egypt?

   _____

   _____

6. What term is given to describe Abraham, Isaac, and Jacob collectively?

   _____

   _____

7. Write two of the Laws of Hammurabi.

   _____

   _____

8. What did the Hyksos introduce to the Egyptians?

   _____

   _____

9. Who is believed to be the pharaoh of the Exodus?

   _____

   _____

10. On the back list the events covered to date in chronological order.

Unification of Egypt—Egypt Falls to Rome
Project—Literature Unit

The Pharaoh's of Ancient Egypt by Elizabeth Payne

The Pharaoh's of Ancient Egypt, by Elizabeth Payne is a wonderful overview of Ancient Egypt starting with Napoleon's campaign in Egypt and the discovery of the Rosetta Stone and ending with Cleopatra and the conquering of Egypt by Rome.

Generally speaking this book can be read independently at the beginning of the year by students in third grade or older and midway through the year by second graders. The following pages have been marked with corresponding flashcard numbers. You may want to use this book as and when you cover the same material on the cards.

UNIFICATION OF EGYPT—EGYPT FALLS TO ROME
Project—Literature Unit

The Pharaoh's of Ancient Egypt by Elizabeth Payne

CHAPTER ONE: *"The Rediscovery of Ancient Egypt"*

1. Who discovered the Rosetta Stone?

_____

2. What is the Rosetta Stone?

_____

_____

3. What did the Rosetta Stone do for history?

_____

_____

4. What proof did historians have that Egypt existed?

_____

_____

5. What do historians today say are the only two reliable ways of learning about a long vanished civilization?

_____

_____

6. How was archaeology born?

_____

_____

7. What were the three languages on the Rosetta Stone?

_____

_____

8. Why was the Rosetta Stone such an important discovery?

_____

_____

UNIFICATION OF EGYPT—EGYPT FALLS TO ROME
Project—Literature Unit

The Pharaoh's of Ancient Egypt by Elizabeth Payne

CHAPTER TWO: *"The First Egyptians and the Dead Demigods"* —Card #6

1. What did archaeologist's discover about early Egyptians when they excavated?

   _____

   _____

2. What does the Nile River do every year?

   _____

   _____

3. What is kemi?

   _____

   _____

4. What impact did irrigation have on the Egyptians?

   _____

   _____

5. What were the three Egyptian kingdoms that developed? Who ruled these kingdoms?

   _____

   _____

6. Where does Egyptian history officially begin?

   _____

   _____

7. What did Egyptians believe about life after death? How did this effect their burial?

   _____

   _____

8. What did the Egyptians consider their Pharaohs to be?

   _____

   _____

UNIFICATION OF EGYPT—EGYPT FALLS TO ROME
Project—Literature Unit

The Pharaoh's of Ancient Egypt by Elizabeth Payne

CHAPTER THREE: *"The Good God--Pharaoh Cheops"* —Card #7

1. For whom was the great pyramid at Giza built?

   _____

   _____

2. How long did it take to build the pyramid at Giza? How many men did it take to build it?

   _____

   _____

3. On the back of this page draw a picture of what the city of Memphis was like at the time of Pharaoh Cheops?

   _____

   _____

4. Why do archaeologists believe Egyptians first wore wigs and used eye paint?

   _____

   _____

5. What was the Great Royal Treasury?

   _____

   _____

6. Did the Egyptians worship one god or many gods?

   _____

   _____

7. What does the Bible tell us about Egyptian gods?

   _____

   _____

Unification of Egypt—Egypt Falls to Rome
Project—Literature Unit

The Pharaoh's of Ancient Egypt by Elizabeth Payne

CHAPTER THREE: *"The Good God--Pharaoh Cheops"* —Card #7

8. What was a mastaba?

_____

_____

9. Who first used stone to build a pharaoh's tomb?

_____

_____

10. Where did the stone come from for the tombs?

_____

_____

11. What tools did the pyramid builders possess?

_____

_____

12. What is one theory as to how the stones were raised into place to build the pyramids?

_____

_____

UNIFICATION OF EGYPT—EGYPT FALLS TO ROME
Project—Literature Unit

The Pharaoh's of Ancient Egypt by Elizabeth Payne

CHAPTER FOUR: *"I Show Thee a Land Topsy-Turvy...."* —Card #'s 8, 14, 18 & 20

1. What important historical information was found inside a mummified crocodile?

   _____

   _____

2. What did some of the scrolls say about Egypt not long after Pharaoh Cheop's death?

   _____

   _____

3. After Cheop's death the nobles and priests grew stronger and bolder.

   What did the priest of Ra do to limit the Pharaoh's power?

   _____

   _____

4. What did the Pharaoh's once devoted nobles do to defy his power?

   _____

   _____

5. What did the nobles begin to say about life after death?

   _____

   _____

6. Who was Osiris?

   _____

   _____

   _____

UNIFICATION OF EGYPT—EGYPT FALLS TO ROME
Project—Literature Unit

The Pharaoh's of Ancient Egypt by Elizabeth Payne

CHAPTER FOUR: *"I Show Thee a Land Topsy-Turvy...."* —Card #'s 8, 14, 18 & 20

7. What actually happened to the central authority in Egypt at this time?

    _____

    _____

8. Who finally brought peace to Egypt once again?

    _____

    _____

9. Who were the Hyksos?

    _____

    _____

10. Who took Egypt back from the Hyksos?

    _____

    _____

11. What two lessons did the valley people learn from the results of the past 1,000 years of history?

    _____

    _____

    _____

UNIFICATION OF EGYPT—EGYPT FALLS TO ROME
Project—Literature Unit

The Pharaoh's of Ancient Egypt by Elizabeth Payne

CHAPTER FIVE: *"His Majesty, Herself--Queen Hatshepsut"*—Card # 22

1. How did Hatshepsut become Pharaoh of Egypt?

   _____

   _____

2. Was there anyone who was not in favor of Hatshepsut being Pharaoh?

   _____

   _____

3. What happened to Thutmose the Third after Hatshepsut seized the throne?

   _____

   _____

4. Who was Senmut?

   _____

   _____

5. What was brought back to Egypt from the trading expedition that Hatshepsut organized?

   _____

   _____

6. What finally happened to Hatshepsut? What part may Thutmose the Third have played in this?

   _____

   _____

   _____

UNIFICATION OF EGYPT—EGYPT FALLS TO ROME
Project—Literature Unit

The Pharaoh's of Ancient Egypt by Elizabeth Payne

CHAPTER SIX: *The Smiter of the Asiatics-Pharaoh Thutmose the Third*

1. What was the Battle of Megiddo?

    _____

    _____

    _____

    _____

2. How were the Syrians finally taken?

    _____

    _____

3. What did Thutmose bring home with him that surprised the Egyptians?

    _____

    _____

4. What did Thutmose do for Amon the King of the Gods and his priesthood?

    _____

    _____

5. Who became Pharaoh at Thutmose's death?

    _____

    _____

6. What is said about Thutmose the Third by historians?

    _____

    _____

7. How was Thutmose's tomb discovered?

    _____

    _____

Unification of Egypt—Egypt Falls to Rome
Project—Literature Unit

The Pharaoh's of Ancient Egypt by Elizabeth Payne

CHAPTER SEVEN: *The Criminal of Akhetaton-Pharaoh Akhnaton*

1. How where the first cuneiform tablets discovered in Egypt?

   _____

   _____

2. Why were the Tell el Amarna tablets important?

   _____

   _____

3. Why was Amenhotep the Third called Amenhotep the Magnificent?

   _____

   _____

4. Who was Amenhotep's wife?

   _____

5. Why did the High Priest of Amon have great political power?

   _____

   _____

6. What new god had risen to prominence at the court of pharaoh?

   _____

   _____

7. Why do many archaeologists believe Amenhotep encouraged worship of the new god, Aton?

   _____

   _____

8. What is meant by Aton was a universal god?

   _____

   _____

   _____

UNIFICATION OF EGYPT—EGYPT FALLS TO ROME
Project—Literature Unit

The Pharaoh's of Ancient Egypt by Elizabeth Payne

CHAPTER SEVEN: *The Criminal of Akhetaton-Pharaoh Akhnaton*

9. Which god did Amenhotep's son, the young Amenhotep, worship?

_____

10. Who was Amenhotep the Third's wife?

_____

_____

11. When was Amenhotep the Third crowned co-regent?

_____

_____

12. What was Akhetaton?

_____

_____

13. Why did Amenhotep the Third change his name of Akhnaton?

_____

_____

14. What was significant about Amenhotep changing his name to Akhnaton?

_____

_____

15. What other changes did Akhnaton make?

_____

_____

_____

_____

UNIFICATION OF EGYPT—EGYPT FALLS TO ROME
Project—Literature Unit

The Pharaoh's of Ancient Egypt by Elizabeth Payne

CHAPTER SEVEN: *The Criminal of Akhetaton-Pharaoh Akhnaton*

16. How did art forms change with Akhaton?

_____

_____

17. Fill in the blank. From the City of the Horizon a decree went forth to all of Egypt, forbidding worship of any god save _____.

18. What problems did the above decree cause?

_____

_____

19. Describe the end of Akhnaton's reign?

_____

_____

_____

20. Who was the next famous pharaoh?

_____

21. Why did Tutankhaton change his name?

_____

22. How old was Tutankhamon when he died?

_____

23. When was Tutankhamon's tomb discovered?

_____

24. Why was Tutankhamon's tomb such an important archeological find?

_____

_____

_____

UNIFICATION OF EGYPT—EGYPT FALLS TO ROME
Project—Literature Unit

The Pharaoh's of Ancient Egypt by Elizabeth Payne

CHAPTER EIGHT: *"The Beginning of the End—Pharaoh Rameses the Second"*—Card # 28, 31 & 32

1. From whom did Rameses the Second inherit the throne of Egypt?

   _____

   _____

2. Who was Rameses son? Who was his grandson?

   _____

   _____

3. Egypt's vast empire had disintegrated under Amenhotep IV's (Akhnaton's) rule.
   What did Rameses the Second do about it?

   _____

   _____

4. Describe the Battle of Kadesh?

   _____

   _____

5. How many wives did Rameses the Second have? What was important about his
   Hittite bride?

   _____

   _____

6. What did Rameses the Second have built?

   _____

   _____

7. How old was Rameses the Second at his death?

   _____

   _____

UNIFICATION OF EGYPT—EGYPT FALLS TO ROME
Project—Literature Unit

The Pharaoh's of Ancient Egypt by Elizabeth Payne

CHAPTER EIGHT: *"The Beginning of the End—Pharaoh Rameses the Second"* —Card # 28, 31 & 32

8. How did the great folk wandering help cause a decline in Egypt?

   What was another name for the "folk wanderers?"

   _____

   _____

9. What happened to Egypt after Rameses the Third's death?

   _____

   _____

10. Who ended the reign of Egypt as an independent country?

    What country gained control of Egypt?

    _____

    _____

11. Who ruled Egypt under the Roman Empire?

    _____

    _____

12. Who seized Egypt in 641 AD? In who's name did they do this?

    _____

    _____

    _____

UNIFICATION OF EGYPT—EGYPT FALLS TO ROME
Project—Literature Unit Answers

The Pharaoh's of Ancient Egypt by Elizabeth Payne

The Rediscovery of Ancient Egypt

1. A company of French soldiers from Napoleon Bonaparte's Egyptian Expeditionary Force.
2. A chunk of polished stone, 2 1/2 ft. across and 3 1/2 ft. high. The flat surface was divided into three sections, each section being engraved with a block of writing. On the top were hieroglyphics, across the bottom was Greek, and in the middle a language recognized.
3. It was the key to the lost history of ancient Egypt. Because the message was written in three languages, hieroglyphics were finally able to be translated.
4. The Bible and Greek and Roman historians, such as Herodotus spoke of Egypt.
5. 1. Being able to read the language. 2. Scientific excavation of buried cities and objects.
6. When an Italian peasant uncovered an ancient wall that was part of Pompeii, people began to dig for objects.
7. 1. hieroglyphs
   2. Demotic
   3. Greek
8. Once we were able to translate the hieroglyphs we were able to learn about Egyptian history. Before this we knew little.

The First Egyptians and the Dead Demigods
Card #6

1. They found that they were small, slender people with dark, wavy hair. They lived by hunting and believed in life after death. They knew this because of what the people buried with them to be used in the next life.
2. Flood its banks.
3. The rich black river-borne silt that was deposited along the river banks every year.
4. It started a chain reaction of causing the people to become more civilized and live in small villages. They no longer spent all their time in search of food as they were able to grow more.
5. 1. Delta of Lower Egypt/Bee King
   2. Middle Egypt/Reed King
   3. Upper Egypt/Hawk King
6. With the first Pharaoh of ancient Egypt Menes.
7. They believed that life would go on much as it had on earth, as long as one's earthly body was preserved. If not a man's spirit would wonder for eternity. Much care was spent preserving the body to be buried.
8. gods

The Good God--Pharaoh Cheops
Card #7

1. Pharaoh Cheops
2. It took 10 years of one hundred thousand men laboring constantly
3. see pages 45-47 for description
4. Wigs to shield their heads from the valley's hot sun, and eye paint to protect against the sun's glare.
5. The place an army of scribes worked keeping Pharaoh's tax lists. They kept lists of those who payed their taxes and checked incoming payments of produce and livestock.
6. Hundreds of deities.
7. That they were false. There is only one true God.
8. A rectangular flat-topped tombs made of brick.
9. Imhotep built a tomb for Pharaoh Zoser.
10. Limestone quarried from valley cliffs.
11. Chisels, copper saws, rope, measuring tapes made of knotted string, sledges and rollers.
12. First the huge blocks of stone were unloaded and dragged to the workshops. There they were measured, cut and bound

Unification of Egypt—Egypt Falls to Rome
Project—Literature Unit Answers

The Pharaoh's of Ancient Egypt by Elizabeth Payne

with ropes. Once bound, they were levered up onto rollers or a sledge. A crew of forty men was then harnessed to the ropes, like horses and ordered to pull the stone. Ramps had been built along the side of the pyramid and the men would pull the stones up to the place they needed to be.

I Show Thee a Land Topsy-Turvy...
Cards #8, 14, 18 & 20
1. Half a dozen ancient papyrus scrolls.
2. They described a land in turmoil.
3. They claimed Pharaoh was the Son of Ra and no longer an independent god. As priest they were the earthly representatives of Ra, so they gained influence.
4. They claimed that estates alloted to them by Pharaoh were not just theirs for their life. Upon their death instead of the land reverting to the crown they began to will it to their heirs.
5. They said that Osiris, god of the dead had promised life after death to every worthy man. It no longer depended on whether or not Pharaoh needed their services in the next life.
6. God of the dead.
7. About 400 years after Cheop's death, the defiant nobles grew so strong that the central authority collapsed. There was period of anarchy, known as the Dark Ages, where little pharaohs were ruling their own domains, casuing division in the valley.
8. Pharaoh Amenemhet
9. An obscure race from the regions of the east.
10. Prince Ahmose who became the first Pharaoh of the eighteenth Dynasty.
11. 1. The time of anarchy convinced them of a need for a strong central government, under a Pharaoh whose divine authority must never be questioned.
2. The Hyksos invasion taught them that their isolated valley was not safe from attack. She needed an army.

His Majesty, Herself—Queen Hatshepsut
Card #22
1. Her little daughter and stepson became Pharaoh and Queen upon her husband's death. After seeming to go along with this one day she just declared herself Pharaoh.
2. Some of Amon priests and some nobles and officials were scandalized at the idea of a woman Pharaoh.
3. He was banished to the gloomy interior of the temple of Amon. His head was shaved, he was given a simple linen kilt and entered training as an apprentice priest.
4. Hatshepsut's chief architect.
5. Myrrh gum, living myrrh trees, ebony, pure ivory, green gold, cinnamon wood, incense, eye paint, apes, monkeys, dogs, skins of southern panthers, natives and their children.
6. She died. Some believe Thutmose broke free, reseized the throne and murdered Hatshepsut.

The Smiter of the Asiatics-Pharaoh Thutmose the Third
1. Thutmose led his men to fight the Syrians. Thutmose led his men into battle "like a flame of fire." He drove his chariot with force and the Syrians just stood and watched Thutmose and his soldiers. Suddenly the Syrians broke ranks and fled.
2. The Syrian soldiers had fled inside their city, even tying their garments into ropes to climb over the locked gates of Megiddo. The soldiers and their families were barricaded behind the walls so the Egyptians decided to

UNIFICATION OF EGYPT—EGYPT FALLS TO ROME
Project—Literature Unit Answers

The Pharaoh's of Ancient Egypt by Elizabeth Payne

starve their enemy into submission. A few weeks later the Syrians surrendered.

3. 2,000 Syrian horses
924 chariots
2,000 cattle
1,921 Asiatic bulls
20,500 additional animals
2,00 prisoners of war

4. He gave Amkon 3 Syrian towns and the right to their taxes. He also gave other land and cattle from the Syrian herd.

5. His son

6. He was history's first general.

7. By three tomb robbers, one whose name was Abderrassul.

The Criminal of Akhetaton-Pharaoh Akhnaton

1. By a peasant woman digging for sebakh, a soil that acts as a fertilizer.

2. They opened the door to a little known time period in Egyptian history, known as the Amarna Heresy.

3. Because of all the vast beautiful building projects he had done. He lived a life of luxury and splendor.

4. Queen Tiy

5. Because of gifts given by prior pharaohs they had enormous wealth.

6. Aton, this new god was the sun itself.

7. It undermined the High Priest of Amon's power.

8. He was a god that could be understood and worshiped by diverse people of vassal states. This god warmed the lands of all people.

9. Aton

10. Nefertiti.

11. When he was about 24 years old, about three years after his marriage.

12. The "City of the Horizon" that Amenhotep the Third built for Aton.

13. He wanted to be associated with Aton and the meant "He who is beneficial of Aton."

14. He was notifying Egypt that Aton had replaced Amon as the crown-supported first god of Egypt.

15. The Amon priesthood was disbanded, Karnark closed and all the temple holdings were to revert to the crown. Amon's name was erased from all monuments or temples. He also abandoned the city of Thebes. The City of the Horizon was to be the new capital of Egypt.

16. They became more lifelike, including the pharaoh. Now longer was pharaoh to be pointed larger than life, but as he was truly seen.

17. Aton.

18. It caused unrest among the people. They were used to worshipping many gods.

19. His mother Tiy came to speak to her son about the unsettledness in Egypt. They argued for days. Tiy won. He fell gravely ill and Nefertiti was banished to live in exile.

20. The nine year old half-brother of Akhnaton, Tutankhaton.

21. The priest of Amon forced him to change it to Tutankhamon.

22. 18

23. November 26, 1922 by Howard Carter.

24. He may have been one of the least important pharaohs, but this tomb appears to have been untouched. It was filled with treasure beyond compare.

UNIFICATION OF EGYPT—EGYPT FALLS TO ROME
Project—Literature Unit Answers

The Pharaoh's of Ancient Egypt by Elizabeth Payne

The Beginning of the End—Pharaoh Rameses the Second
Card #28, 31 & 32

1. Pharaoh Haremhab, Rameses was his vizier.
2. Seti, Ramses the Second
3. He retook lands lost by prior pharaohs.
4. Remeses was left alone to face 2,500 Hittite charioteers, with only his personal bodyguard to defend him. He tied his reins around his waist to leave his hands free and charged forth. Eventually his men came to his aid and began to fight. The battle ended and Rameses claimed himself a victory even though he had not captured the city.
5. 7 Great Royal wives and untold numbers of secondary wives. His marriage to his Hittite bride sealed a treaty signed 16 years earlier with the Hittites.
6. A new capital he called Tanis.
7. 85
8. They invaded the lands and the Egyptians fought for a while and then seemed to give up. / Indo-Europeans
9. Egypt suffered a series of disastrously low floods causing famine to be severe.
10. Alexander the Great. Greece.
11. Queen Cleopatra
12. The Arabs in the name of their prophet Mohammed.

EGYPTIAN DECOR
Project

Bulletin Board Pattern

Have students color and cut out this figure to use as a border around a bulletin board.

EGYPTIAN LIFE
Project—An Egyptian Feast

The Egyptian people enjoyed their food. Wouldn't it be a fun activity to prepare an Egyptian Feast? Following you will find some recipes of foods similar to that which the ancient Egyptians enjoyed. Of course they are much easier for us to prepare due to modern conveniences.

Choose a day for your feast and send out invitations to the parents of the students or friends inviting them to the feast. You may even want to have everyone come in costume. And you may want to assign everyone a recipe to share with the class (as in a covered dish supper).

EGYPTIAN LIFE
*Project—*An Egyptian Feast

Basboussa *(Egyptian Pastry)*

This sweet, melt-in-your-mouth pastry can be made several days ahead, covered with plastic wrap and refrigerated. Bring to room temperature before serving. Try serving it with a fruit compote, fresh fruit or sorbet.

1/2 pound unsalted butter (2 sticks)

1 pound semolina flour* (about 2 3/4 cups)

1 cup sugar

1 cup coconut flakes

1 teaspoon baking powder

1 cup milk

1 cup pine nuts

For syrup:

1 cup sugar

1/2 cup water

1 tablespoon lemon juice

2 teaspoons vanilla extract

Sold in speciality stores.

Preheat oven to 350 degrees. Grease a 9x13 inch baking pan. Melt butter and mix with semolina, sugar, coconut, baking powder and milk. Sprinkle pine nuts over top. Spoon into baking pan and bake for 30 minutes or until golden on top.

For syrup, add sugar and water to a saucepan with a heavy bottom. Warm over medium heat until sugar completely dissolves. Do not let the liquid boil before the sugar is dissolved. Bring to a boil for 5 minutes or until thick. The syrup should remain clear. Remove from heat and stir in lemon juice and vanilla.

When pastry is baked, remove from oven and cut into 1-1/2 inch squares. Spoon hot syrup over the top. It should drip through to permeate the cake. Makes 8 servings (24 squares).

EGYPTIAN LIFE
Project—An Egyptian Feast

Pita Bread Stuffed with Honey, Dates and Almonds
Ingredients

Pkg. of Pita Bread

1 egg white

sesame seeds

1 eight ounce box pitted dates

2 tbsps. honey

4 oz. almonds

    Brush one side of pita bread with egg white, then sprinkle with sesame seeds. If you want, you may brown sesame seeds first in the oven. Before you put it in the oven, cut pita in half and then quarters if so desired. Place pita on cookie sheet and bake at 350 degrees for about five minutes. The sesame seeds will be glued to the pita. When you remove from oven, open up the pockets and let them cool.

    Put dates, honey and almonds in a blender to chop and mix. Stuff the pita bread with this mixture.

Egyptian Life
Project—An Egyptian Feast

Date Nut Bars
Ingredients

1 cup granulated sugar

1/2 cup butter softened

2 eggs, well beaten

3/4 cup flour

1/4 tsp. baking powder

1 tsp. vanilla

1 cup dates (chopped finely)

1 cup almonds

Cream butter and sugar, add eggs, then flour and baking powder. Add vanilla, then dates and nuts. Put into a well greased 9 by 9 inch pan, spread enough to cover pan. Bake in 325 degree oven 15 to 20 minutes. Cut in one and one half inch squares while still warm.

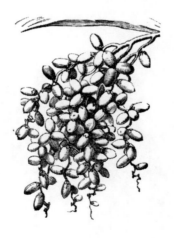

EGYPTIAN LIFE
Project—An Egyptian Feast

Caramelized Fish
Ingredients

2 pounds fish fillet (any white fish will do)

1 medium onion, sliced

1/4 cup honey

salt and pepper to taste

1/4 cup olive oil

1/4 cup butter

Melt butter, add onion, sauté onion. Add honey and cook until caramelized, stirring constantly. Remove from heat and set aside.

Rub fish filets with olive oil, then salt and pepper to taste. Pour remaining oil in pan. Pan fry fish until white and firm. Pour caramelized onions over fish and heat until bubbly, white and firm. It usually takes about 5 minutes per side depending on the thickness of the fillet. Pour caramelized onions over the top. Heat until bubbly and serve.

Fruit Plate
The Egyptians had both green and red grapes. They also had some kinds of melons. Cut up melon slices and grapes for a fruit platter.

ANCIENT EGYPT
Project–Example History-Grammar Sentences

DIRECTIONS FOR HISTORY-GRAMMAR INTEGRATION

We recommend the Shurley Grammar program as being the one which does the best job of teaching students the fundamental structure of the English sentence. Obviously, the sentences in the various sentences groups of Shurley are not all going to have any relationship with the content of their history, but we believe that making up extra practice sentences which have content culled from their history lessons can bring a beneficial "synergy" into the curriculum.

Several sentences derived from the content of the history lessons have been written and parsed as examples. Obviously, the possibilities are limitless.

It would also be worthwhile to have the children make up their own, history-related sentences. This could be done for the whole class to parse, or for their own, individual practice and improved sentences that are integral to the Shurley lessons.

```
             A    ADJ    SN     /   V    P    A   OP
1.  SN V     The ancient Egyptians / lived (along the Nile).
    D P1
```

1. The ancient Egyptians lived along the Nile.
2. Who lived along the Nile? Egyptians/SN
3. What is being said about Egyptians? Egyptians lived/V
4. Along/P
5. Along what? Nile/OP
6. The/A
7. The/A
8. What kind of Egyptians? ancient/Adj
9. SN V P1 check
10. (along the Nile), prepositional phrase
11. Period, statement/D
12. Go back to the verb; divide the complete subject from the complete predicate

ANCIENT EGYPT
Project—Example History-Grammar Sentences

```
        A     SN     P  OP     V     P       OP
2. SN V   The Unification (of Egypt) / began (under Pharaoh Menes).
   P1 D
```

1. The unification of Egypt began under Pharaoh Menes.
2. What began under Pharaoh Menes? unification/SN
3. What is being said about unification? unification began/V
4. Under/P
5. Under whom? Pharaoh Menes/OP
6. The/A
7. Of/P
8. Of what? Egypt/OP
9. SN V P1 check
10. (of Egypt), prepositional phrase
11. (under Pharaoh Menes), prepositional phrase
12. period, statement/D
13. Go back to the verb; divide the complete subject from the complete predicate.

```
          P     A      OP          ADJ  SN  P1    V     P  ADJ  OP
3. SN V   (During the Intermediate Periods), rival pharaohs / fought (with each other). D
```

1. During the Intermediate Periods, rival pharaohs fought with each other.
2. Who fought with each other? pharaohs/SN
3. What is being said about pharaohs? pharaohs fought/V
4. With/P
5. With whom? other/OP
6. What kind of other? each/Adj
7. During/P
8. During what? Intermediate Periods/OP
9. The/A
10. SN V P1 check
11. (during the Intermediate Periods), prepositional phrase
12. (with each other), prepositional phrase
13. Period, statement/D
14. Go back to the verb; divide the complete subject from the complete predicate.

Ancient Egypt
Project—Example History-Grammar Sentences

```
            A    ADJ    SN    V    P  OP    P   OP
4.  SN V    The fierce Hyksos / rode (to war) (in chariots).D
    P1
```

1. The fierce Hyksos rode to war in chariots.
2. Who rode to war in chariots? Hyksos/SN
3. What is being said about Hyksos? Hyksos rode/V
4. To/P
5. To what? war/OP
6. In/P
7. In what? chariots/OP
8. The/A
9. What kind of Hyksos? fierce/Adj
10. SN V P1 check
11. (to war), prepositional phrase
12. (in chariots), prepositional phrase
13. Period, statement/D
14. Go back to the verb; divide the complete subject from the complete predicate.

```
            SN       V    P OP       P   OP
5.  SN V    Egypt / fell (to Rome) (in 30 BC).D
    P1
```

1. Egypt fell to Rome in 30 BC.
2. What fell to Rome in 30 BC? Egypt/SN
3. What is being said about Egypt? Egypt fell/V
4. To/P
5. To What? Rome/OP
6. In/P
7. In what? 30 BC/OP
8. SN V P1 check
9. (to Rome), Prepositional phrase
10. (in 30 BC), Prepositional Phrase
11. Period, statement/D
12. Go back to the verb; divide the complete subject from the complete predicate.

HISTORY FACTS

Card Name: _____

Card Number: _____

Who:

_____

_____

What:

_____

_____

_____

_____

_____

_____

_____

_____

_____

Where:

_____

_____

When:

_____

_____

_____

CHAPTER SUMMARY

Event:

Date:
Who
What

Where

GREAT GAMES FOR HISTORY REVIEW

Make cards with names, dates, events and places to keep in a packet. Add to the cards as more topics are studied. On review days pull out the 3x5 cards for ready made clues. They can be helpful for many of the following games, especially when everyone's brains are tired and they just can't think of a word for *hangman* or a *charade* to act out.

Who Am I? (Where Am I? What Am I?)

A Student selects a person, place or thing from their history knowledge. The student who is "It" gives clues and calls on classmates (with their hands raised) to guess. The student with the correct guess gets the next turn to be "It."

Twenty Questions

The student chooses a history person, place or thing. They announce to the class whether they are a person, place or thing. The class can ask twenty questions. All questions must be worded so that a 'yes' or a 'no' answer is given. If after twenty questions no one has guessed the correct answer, "It" identifies the person, place or thing.

Charades

Play as individuals or as teams. One person or team acts out clues to an identity or event. The remaining students or team tries to guess. Set a time limit of several minutes.

Thumbs Up or Down

The teacher asks 'yes' or 'no' questions pertaining to history. The class responds with thumbs up for yes and thumbs down for no.

Knock-Knock

Teacher says, "Knock-Knock." Student replies "Who's there?" Teacher gives a fact as response. For example, "I had six wives." Student tells the name, "King Henry VIII."

Mixed-Up Story

Retell a historical event with a few facts incorrect. As the teacher tells the story, students raise their hands and correct the errors.

Chronological Order

Give the students one or two history flashcards. Have the students place their cards in the chronological order without looking at the numbers on the back.

A, B, C's of History

The first student begins by naming a history person, place or thing that begins with an A and telling a fact about it. The next student follows in turn with the next letter of the alphabet. For example, A-Aristotle was a philosopher. B-Botticelli was a Renaissance artist.

Ball Toss

Teacher tosses a small soft ball to a student who answers the question posed. The student tosses the ball back to the teacher.

Baseball

This can be adapted to paper for smaller groups or for quieter times. Chair baseball can be quite noisy, but will probably be the class' favorite review game. Set up chairs in a baseball diamond. Label home, 1st, 2nd, and 3rd bases. Divide the class into two teams. Player gets a hit when they correctly answer a question. They can move around the bases as their team mates correctly answer. A run is scored when the players advance to home. Incorrect answers are outs.

GREAT GAMES
Page 2

Tic Tac Toe
This can be played in pairs or by dividing into two teams. Students choose where to place the X or O when they correctly answer a question.

Secret Identity
One player selects a person and tells other players the initial of the selection's last name. Other players ask questions phrased so that the chooser has to identify other people with the same initial. If the initial is H for example, the first question could be "Are you a president of the United States?" The response may be, "No, I am not William Harrison." If the chooser is stumped for a response with the proper initial, then the asker can request other information: "Are you alive?" The "stumped" questions can only be answered by a 'yes' or a 'no.' The chooser continues answering questions until someone guesses the identity.

Boxes
Set up the game with a square grid made up of dots. Ask questions of the students. Correct answers earn a horizontal or vertical line connecting two of the dots. The student who closes in a box puts his initials inside and gets another turn. He may continue adding lines as long as each line forms a new box. The Student with the most boxes wins.

Categories
Select twenty categories ahead of time (colonies, items traded with England, Presidents, founding fathers, famous ships, items England taxed). Each student writes names of all the categories across the top of his paper. The players have 5-10 minutes to write as many items that fit the categories as they can. When time is up, trade lists for scoring. Each correct answer is one point. An answer no one else has gets two points. The player with the most points wins.

Drawing in the Dark
Retell a history event to the class. The class should draw the events with their eyes closed. Judges can choose the most accurate, funniest, etc.

Hangman
Choose words related to history. Each student guesses a letter in turn until someone has a guess or the stickman figure is hanged.

Magazing
Collect as many old magazines as feasible. Allow students several minutes to depict a historical event by cutting out pictures and words from magazines and gluing them to blank pages. They can even compile the pages into a book to show the flow of events.

Questions
The first player asks a question. The second player must respond with another related question, and then the first player with a question, etc. If a player pauses too long between questions, forgets to ask a question, or asks a nonsensical question, he is out. For example, "Did Paul Revere live in Boston?" "Didn't he look for a signal in the church tower?" "Was it one if by land, two if by sea?"

OLD TESTAMENT/ANCIENT EGYPT
Veritas Press History Song

First came creation, seven days, listen to what God did, He created everything and this is how it went...

Day one day and night, Day two heaven and earth, Day three seas and land, Day four sun, moon and stars, Day five creatures of the sky and of the sea, Day six creatures of dry land and then came man. Then God saw that it was good, all of His creation, so he took the seventh day and on that day He rested.

2nd came the Fall in the Garden of Eden,
3rd was Cain and Abel,
4th the Earth was Flooded,
5th came the Tower of Babel,
6th the Unification of Upper and Lower Egypt by Pharaoh Menes.

7 the Old Kingdom in Egypt,
8 the First Intermediate Period,
9 The Call of Abram,
10 God's Covenant with Abraham.

11 Hagar and Ishmael,
12 was Sodom and Gomorrah,
13 The Birth and Sacrifice of Abrahams son named Isaac,
14 The Middle Kingdom,
15 Joseph as a Slave,
16 The Famine in Egypt,
Then came number seventeen.

God gave Isaac's son named Jacob twelve sons of his own. They became the patriarchs of all the tribes of Israel. Rueben, Simeon, Levi—Judah, Issachar, Zebulun, Joseph and brother Benjamin, still four more left to name. Dan and brother Naphtali, Gad and Asher, this is why God gave Jacob twelve sons and from them He made a great nation.

18 came the Second Intermediate Period in Egypt,
19 came a list of laws, The Code of Hammurabi.

20 the Hyksos invaded Egypt,
21 The Early New Kingdom,
22 The Birth of Moses,
23 The Plagues in Egypt,
24 came the Exodus in 1446 B.C.

25 The Ten Commandments,
26 Pharaoh Amenhotep, worshipped only one god. This was monotheism.
27 came the famous reign of Pharaoh Tutankamon,
28 came the Later New Kingdom, The Golden Age in Egypt,
29 The Davidic Kingdom 1011 B.C.,
30 came the Reign of Solomon - Builder of the temple,
31 came Alexander, Alexander the Great, he led Greece in conquering Egypt in 332 B.C.

Number 32 was last but certainly not least, Egypt fell to Roman rule and so came to an end. Egypt fell to Roman rule and so came to an end.